Why Uniform Civil Code?

P.S. Bisht
P.K. Sharma

Copyright © 2020 Prem Singh Bisht.

All rights reserved. No Part of this publication may be reproduced, distributed, or transmitted in any form or by any means, including photocopying, recording, or other electronic or mechanical methods, without prior written permission of the copyright owner, except in the case of brief quotations embodied in critical reviews and certain other non-commercial uses permitted by copyright law. For permission requests, write to the copyright owner, addressed as under.

ISBN: 979-8-6678-9147-5

Edited by Abhinav Singh Bisht
First printing edition July 2020.

Correspondence Address:
1157, Sector 21
Gurugram, Haryana
India, 122016

THIS WORK

IS

DEDICATED TO

MY FAMILY, FRIENDS

AND

NATION

FOREWORD

About this book:

In this Book an attempt has been made by the authors to deeply probe the paramount question we are facing in contemporary Indian scenario i.e "How far the need for implementation of Uniform Civil Code is necessary in a fast globalising world and what are the constraints involved in doing so?"
The authors have endeavoured to focus on studying the development of various Personal Laws in their historical perspective. India being a large geographical and demographical entity, is blessed with multi-cultural, multi-lingual, multi-religious and multi-racial features making it a sub-continent. This unity in diversity is its unique feature but it also creates several issues to be resolved amicably within the framework of the Constitution of India. The authors have further stretched to embark on the legislative efforts made by the law makers since independence in the direction of realising the constitutional commitment of Uniform Civil Code.
The Judicial trends reflected in the various pronouncements of the Supreme Court, related to matters pertaining to conflicting issues of Personal Laws were also looked into by the authors, revealing that on several occasions' desirability of the enactment of Uniform Civil Code has been expressed. The authors describe how in modern day parlance, in a democratic society upholding the fundamental rights, gender equality and abolition of discrimination of all kinds are the key factor for binding

a nation in a more cohesive way. An attempt has also been made to analyse pros and cons of the issue at hand in the light of socio- religio- legal matrix.

We know that the domain of personal law comprises of those laws which apply to a specific class or group of people based on their religious faith and culture. A dire necessity to reform Family Law based on conflicting issues pertaining to Marriage and Divorce, Custody and Guardianship, Adoption and Maintenance & Succession and Inheritance is being long felt. In India we belong to different castes and religions having a distinct faith and belief system. The irony is if Personal Laws are governed by Article 13 and Article 372 of the Constitution, then they will be void to the extent that they would be in contravention of Article 14, 15 and 21 of the Constitution. It is in this light of Constitutional provisions the debate surrounding the enactment of Article 44 has to be examined. However, it will be an uphill task for our parliamentarians to reach at an amicable solution in resolving the issue at hand. At this stage we can only hope that the debate surrounding the enactment of Article 44 may generate more light than heat.

The Book comprises of six Chapters. Chapter 1 offers a General Overview about Uniform Civil Code. Chapter 2 deals with the Historical Perspective of Uniform Civil Code by manifesting on the approach of the Personal Laws and the initiatives taken after Independence. Chapter 3 deals with the International Perspective and the current trends pertaining to Uniform Civil Code. Chapter 4 starts with Constituent Assembly Debates and embarks on the recent initiatives with new frontiers and

Legislative Reforms. Chapter 5 deals with Judicial Perspective and trends wherein a number of case laws have been discussed. Chapter 6 while concluding gives Suggestions thereby triggering a debate on the issue in the direction of seeking an amicable settlement.

In a nutshell, time is ripe for discovering the connection between diversity and uniformity in our Personal Laws, so that on the parameter of upholding the basic fundamental rights, while keeping in mind the secular fabric of our Constitution, the issue of Uniform Civil Code can be addressed. In the end, we must appreciate that Laws are never static as they evolve with the passage of time to meet the changing needs and aspiration of society. Also, it wouldn't be out of place to say that all Laws world over are a product of temporal and spatial variable.

I must complement the authors for having so analytically discussed the entire issue. I am sure that this book will be of immense value to those who are interested in a critical study of Constitutional Law.

Maj Gen AB Gorthi, AVSM, VSM (Retd),
Former Judge Advocate General and Administrative Member CAT

PREFACE

Preface to the First Edition:

This book is based on my work as a legal researcher. As a former Civil Servant (I.P.S.) I had the unique opportunity to see various issues that plague the Indian society. Nevertheless, it was a humbling task during my research to understand and read about complex human set-ups and quests for greater good. While this book does not aim to question the legitimacy of any of these quests, it does question the extent to which old customs should play a role in modern pluralistic society. This book is, in fact, an outcome of my experience as a Law enforcer as well as a student interested in legal studies for the last several years.

The book aims to instill with its various arguments a debate on implementation of Uniform Civil Code (UCC). In order to keep the content of this book to suit a light reading I have limited the arguments around four major issues: marriages, divorce, inheritance and position of women. The book is written to bring readers up to speed with evolution and manner of adaptation of various Personal Laws in India. It enquires the nature of the need to implement UCC that has been felt in the under-represented parts of society as well as the legal institutions.

Keeping this in view, the present book has been written with two clear objectives, viz., (i) to enable researchers/common people , irrespective of their field of interest to ponder upon the desirability of the enactment of Uniform Civil Code in the present day scenario; and (ii) to acquaint the reader with the background of the issue envisaged in the Constitution, in order to deliberate upon the issue with an open mind.

The book has a total of six chapters, each of these chapters begin with a general backdrop to sink the reader into the theme of the chapter. These themes range from a Constitutional debate to legal, historical and international perspectives. The book starts with an overview of the values of the Indian Constitution and its various salient features, with Uniform Civil Code in focus. It further introduces the reader to various academic work already carried out by scholars and continues to highlight the importance of the UCC debate in a political setting.

The book visits historical events that have introduced various cultures to the Indian subcontinent. With main focus on evolution of Personal Laws as we know them today. Chapter two has been dedicated to make the reader understand how some customs remain un-codified till date. The chapter gives an account of challenges ahead of the Constitution makers at the time of its making. This chapter will lay a strong historical background of the legal challenges that Indian society faces today.

Chapter three delves into a more theoretical approach, it introduces the reader to relevant thinkers to understand the social construct of norms and legal systems. An attempt has been made to exemplify the constraints discrepancy in legal systems bring in an international setting. The chapter further illustrates recent media reports, it concludes with India's stand on state's interference in religious affairs and the delicate equilibrium that must be struck to bring about the necessary legislation.

Chapter four tracks the debate surrounding UCC at the time of Constitutional Assembly and the efforts made in the same direction after the Constitution came into force. It highlights some key cases by which Courts have pointed the legislatures towards legislative reforms. Chapter five recalls several sensational cases where the courts have pointed out the need to implement a UCC. The trends show how justice is delayed and long legal battles must be fought by a justice seeker before securing their Fundamental Rights. The book aims to point challenges before the UCC makers that must be met before bringing such legislation. In the last chapter I have concluded the book with some suggestions.

It is hoped that the book shall provide assistance to all those who are interested in the research studies of one sort or the other. I am also grateful to all those persons whose writings and works have inspired me during the preparation phase of this book. I am equally grateful to the reviewer of the manuscript of this book who made extremely valuable suggestions and has thus contributed in enhancing the standard of the book. I shall feel amply rewarded if the book proves helpful in initiating a fruitful dialogue between the learned academia and respective stakeholders on the subject of the desirability of enacting Uniform Civil Code. The objective of discussion should be to bind the Nation in a more cohesive way than ever before. Thereby, realising the dream of one Nation, one code.

I look forward to suggestions from all readers, specially from experienced researchers and scholars for further improving the subject content as well as the presentation of this book.

P. S. Bisht
Former I.P.S.

PREFACE

Since the thoughts behind the words matter a lot, therefore, at the outset this Book invests in stirring the on-going debate of securing a common law for all the citizens. Though a System of any kind, in any context, generally resists change, advocating the established practice and preserving the status quo but with changing times, system should also change. The inertia of changed mind- set often navigates towards the spark of change for betterment. Having spent more than 40 years in the field of law and legal studies, I feel fortunate to share knowledge, observations and analysis through this Book, which may act as a catalyst for promoting awareness among the general public and initiating the decision, which in turn, may entail a desirable social change thus, embracing a better tomorrow. An awakened and a vigilant society will be a benefit for the Nation, providing a thrust for a positive transformation. The Book reflects two different levels. Firstly, it may be read by people having a limited legal background and secondly, by legal scholars and political thinkers as it caters for their interest, giving rise to fine ideologies worth for the Nation's development.

A distinctive feature of the Book is that the journey can be started from any Chapter with which one gets enthralled, based on one's interests, tastes and preferences, therefore, not sticking to the normal sequential textbook structure reading. Everyone is not expected to agree with the content and ideas put forth in the Book, but it is hoped that the information and knowledge presented will be a wakeup call for the general public, regulatory agencies, legislators, political and religious leaders as well as social workers.

The Book comprises of six Chapters. Chapter 1 offers a General Overview about Uniform Civil Code. Chapter 2 deals with the Historical Perspective of Uniform Civil Code by manifesting on the approach of the Personal Laws and the initiatives taken after Independence. Chapter 3 deals with the International Perspective and the current trends pertaining to Uniform Civil Code. Chapter 4 starts with Constituent Assembly Debates and embarks on the recent initiatives with new frontiers and Legislative Reforms. Chapter 5 deals with Judicial Perspective and trends wherein a number of case laws have been discussed. Chapter 6 while concluding gives Suggestions thereby triggering a debate on the issue in the direction of seeking an amicable settlement.

I hope this Book is widely read. To avoid the unsuccessful attempts of the past, we need to move in the direction of consensus as one Nation. We need to follow the edifice created by the forefathers of the Indian Constitution in the shape of Article 44. Now is the right time.

Maj Gen PK Sharma (Retd)
Professor & Director
Amity Law School and
Dean Faculty of Law, AUH

CONTENTS

The book is organized in six chapters, the content of chapters is as mentioned below:

CHAPTER I INTRODUCTION	
1.1 Introductory Note	1
1.2 General Overview	6
CHAPTER II HISTORICAL PERSPECTIVE OF UNIFORM CIVIL CODE	
2.1 General	18
2.2 Historical Perspective of Personal Law	21
2.3 Initiative After Independence	29
2.4 Conclusion	32
CHAPTER III INTERNATIONAL PERSPECTIVE AND CURRENT TRENDS	
3.1 International Scenario	35
3.2 Current Scenario and Media Reports	43
3.3 Conclusion	49

CHAPTER IV
LEGISLATIVE PERSPECTIVE AND BACKGROUND

4.1 General	51
4.2 Constituent Assembly Debates	52
4.3 Legislative Efforts Since 1950	58
4.4 Recent Initiatives in this Direction	63
4.5 New Frontiers of Legislative Reforms	72
4.6 Conclusion	77

CHAPTER V
JUDICIAL PERSPECTIVE AND TRENDS

5.1 General	78
5.2 Narasu Appa Mali case	81
5.3 Shah Bano Begam case	82
5.4 Jorden Diengdeh V. S.S Chopra case	84
5.5 Sarla Mudgal v Union of India case	86
5.6 Ahmadabad Women's Action Group (AWAG) v. Union of India	89
5.7 Seema v Aswani Kumar	93
5.8 Vishwa Lochan Madan V. Union of India	93

5.9 Shayara Bano v. Union of India case	94
5.10 Kantaru Rajeevaru v. Indian Young Lawyers Association and ors (Sabarimala case):	95
5.11 An insight to Judicial Pronouncements and Personal Laws	95
5.12 Recent Media reports	102
5.13 Conclusion	105
CHAPTER VI **CONCLUSION AND SUGGESTIONS**	
6.1 Conclusion	111
6.2 Suggestions	129
References	134

CHAPTER I
INTRODUCTION

1.1 INTRODUCTORY NOTE:

The people of India gave themselves a Republic which is Sovereign, Socialist, secular and Democratic with a Constitutional system having focus on Justice, Liberty, Equality and Fraternity. These principles are deeply embodied in a set of institutions and laws, conventions and practices. It was the wisdom of our founding fathers that they took cognizance of an external reality. Today India with a population of well over 1.3 billion compromises of about 4635 communities, out of which 78 percent are not only linguistic and cultural but social categories. Religious minorities constitute 19.4 percent of the total. It is interesting to note that human diversities are hierarchical as well as spatial. India is a plural society[1] and a culture imbued with considerable doses of syncretism. It is this plurality that the Constitution endowed with a democratic polity and a secular state structure. India being a multiethnic, multi-cultural, multi-lingual, multi-racial and multi-religious country is a

---

[1] *Why Pluralism and Secularism are essential for our democracy: Vice President*, PIB Archives, 6 August 2017

secular state with no state-owned religion. It gives equal protection to all religions. Religions are governed by their own Personal Laws and practices. Consequently, the conditions for marriage, divorce, adoption, inheritance, maintenance, etc vary from religion to religion resulting in several complicated issues and matrimonial conflicts. Article 44 of Indian Constitution[2] provides that "State shall endeavor to secure for its citizens a Uniform Civil Code throughout the territory of India". Article 44 being a Directive Principle of State Policy is not enforceable, but it is the positive duty of state as a moral obligation. Although many jurists, academia and people tend to favor and support the Uniform Civil Code but there is a lack of consensus and lack of a strong political will. India has a long history of Personal Laws, which cannot be surrendered so easily. It necessitates to draw a broad consensus among different communities and classes to pave the way for a Uniform Civil Code. India is a secular nation since time immemorial. However, due to modernization and globalization today, the meaning of secularism particularly in relation to social affairs of Indian society may need to be re-conceptualized. Therefore, many are of the opinion that time has come to ponder upon the concept of secularism in Indian context and also to get rid of age old un-democratic Personal Laws, in order to strive to attain national integration through enacting Uniform Civil Code on a priority basis. According to some it will usher in a new era of One Nation One Code, but it has to be examined in the light

---

[2] Constitution of India Part IV, Article 44

Chapter I: Introduction

of the fact that can a Uniform Civil Code work for all in India?

The codification of laws in Indian context dates back to colonial time. The legislative literature of India being shaped by its colonial masters by plays an important role. The Lex Loci Report [3], of 1840 recommended the requirement for codification of Indian laws concerning crime, evidence and contract but did not interfere with the personal laws of different communities by keeping them outside the purview of codification process. Here, the term Lex Loci stands for the place (*locus*) where the crime was committed and defines which law (*lex*) the crime should be viewed through. Warren Hastings in 1780, in Administration of Justice[4] Regulation made it clear that disputes arising out of family matters, must be governed by the respective personal laws of communities concerned as a policy declaration. Therefore, Britishers merely codified the law dealing with crime on secular line. In post-colonial time in the backdrop of partition perhaps the society was not well educated and ready for this change. Therefore, when the Constitution was in the making it seems to prevent our legislature in dealing with this sensitive issue of religious practices law as a wise decision. Now the question is how far with enhanced educational and awareness level the modern Indian society is ready for this change?

---

[3] Report of first law commission 31, October 1840

[4] Indian Legal History 2006 by M.P. Jain

India is a country with a rich cultural heritage, which has assimilated a vast variety of religions, cultures, traditions and languages within its fold. This is why, India is not only a country but a sub-continent as it stands out distinctly from the rest of the continent. It has both intrinsic unity as well as extrinsic plurality and diversity arising out of a number of forces such as religion, region, caste, creed, language, habitat, etc. Constitution of India promotes and protects intrinsic unity in a diversity rich country. The partition of the country on the basis of religion has left deep rooted wounds, making the task of protecting its unity really challenging. At the time of drafting of our constitution word secularism was not inserted in the preamble but Article 25 to 30 of our constitution provided the essence of secularism by making it omnipresent in essence. Thus, Part III of the constitution[5], comprising of fundamental rights, is woven around the idea of secularism. The term secularism was inserted in the preamble by 42nd Amendment[6] Act 1976, thereby making secularism an integral part of the basic structure of the Indian Constitution. The term secularism was inserted in order to counter the undercurrent of communalism and preventing any kind of confusion regarding secular nature of Indian Constitution. The constitution guarantees to its citizens freedom of religion and conscience, and also restrains the state from making any discriminatory treatment on the basis of religion. One nation, one Constitution, one citizenship, one national

---

[5] Constitution of India part III.

[6] The Constitution (Forty-second amendment) Act 1976.

anthem, are some of the salient features of Indian Constitution. The debate surrounding Uniform Civil Code is often related to the issues of secularism and national integrity[7]. In legal Parlance, Uniform Civil Code stands for *"administration of a set of civil laws to govern all people without any discrimination of religion"*. The common areas under Uniform Civil Code consist of marriage, divorce, adoption and inheritance. It is asserted by some scholars that lack of common Civil Code adversely affects the life of Indian women. The recent example of bringing in a legislation on triple *talaq* (*talaq-e-biddh*) as illegal and unconstitutional on 30 July 2019 by Parliament of India is an effort in this direction.

India as a nation is known for a land of cultural diversity, multiple languages, and religions. Diversity is appreciated but India as a nation has often faced problems of integration and governance due to this factor, because different code governs, different communities coupled with different religions, customs, tradition and usage. If we go by Constitution, it envisaged a Uniform Civil Code under Article 44, bringing in its ambit a large number of personal laws. However, despite of multiple challenges India has achieved successfully uniform legislation in almost every sphere of national life i.e civil, contractual, criminal etc, except family and matrimonial laws. Perhaps this is why the framers of the Constitution made provisions under Article 44 to empower the state with this responsibility in time to come when the nation will be

---

[7] Tahir Mahmood, personal Laws in Crisis, p.3 (1986)

prepared for it. However, during Constitutional assembly debate due to lack of consensus to arrive at a common ideology this Article was reduced to a mere directive in nature rather than mandatory. The talk on Uniform Civil Code are going on since independence and particularly from Constitutional Assembly Debate time. The judiciary through its various pronouncement has been playing a proactive role to enforce Uniform Civil Code. This has been criticized as a Judicial overreach but by and large it has been appreciated by Indian masses of varied background, which is a positive sign. As Supreme Court has asked Union Government regarding its willingness to enact a Uniform Civil Code, in order to override age old inconsistent personal laws of different religious groups. Despite of an ongoing heated debate on Uniform Civil Code one thing is undisputed and clear that any provision of personal law which abridges or violate the fundamental rights stands unconstitutional as per Article 13, of the Part III of the Constitution[8] and so it must be struck down. Besides, this inherent inconsistency in various personal laws has also been challenged on the grounds of Article 14, which guarantees the Right to Equality.

1.2 GENERAL OVERVIEW

Keeping in view of the above context and historical and legal background any person of common prudence will be confronted with a question, whether there is a need of implementing a Uniform Civil Code at the present point

---

[8] supra note 4

of time for achieving the social unity and solidarity of India as envisaged in the Preamble of the Constitution of India? Another aspect is to seek probing questions and answers regarding the problems and challenges in enacting legislation in this regard. Not only this but also to probe into the nature of the proposed legislation and its consequences, beside studying Personal Laws from a different viewpoint.

It will be worthwhile to ponder upon certain studies, having relevance to the issue, including the work done by legal scholars in the field as well as on-going efforts made by the Ministry of Law and Legislative Affair, Law Commission of India and Judicial observation in this regard. Some of the work done by scholars related to subject matter of Uniform Civil Code is worthwhile to be summarized as:

•*Dr Parminder Kaur (2011)* [9] published a paper on *personal laws of India vis-a-vis Uniform Civil Code* in the International Monthly Journal I.S.S.N. 23216417. The study lamented that Indian Muslim Law cannot be allowed to remain outside the Constitution, but it needs to be carefully assimilated.

•*Dr Manoj Kumar and Ms Shalini Shukla (2012)*[10] also undertook a similar research study titled *Personal Law vis-a-vis Uniform Civil Code*. India is a country with a

---

[9] International Monthly Journal I.S.S.N. 23216417

[10] Dr Manoj Kumar and Ms Shalini Shukla (2012)

rich cultural heritage which has assimilated a vast variety of religions, cultures, traditions and languages within it's fold. The outcome was that the introduction of uniform civil code in India lies in the hands of its religious masses as well as religious leaders. It can be achieved only if Indian community at large is mature enough to accept Uniform civil code which will govern their personal issues.

•*Chintaman Rout (2013)*[11] undertook a research study regarding *Uniform Civil Code and Gender Justice*: an analysis under customary law. The objective of the study was to discover the effect of Uniform Civil Code on Gender Equality. According to researcher key areas for women empowerment are social status, gender bias, health, security both social as well as economic. He also highlighted the fact that there is no Uniform Civil Code in India, but a Uniform Criminal Code does exist, which is equally applicable to all Indian nationals irrespective of their religion. But there is no uniformity as far as Personal laws are concerned. He went to the comparison of Hindu law and Muslim law to identify the discrimination against women. Scholar in his study on analysis of Uniform Civil Code and Gender Justice[12] under customary law, located disparity in the rights of Christian as well as Parsi women. The study concluded with an observation that no Gender Justice is possible unless the women, irrespective of their religious

---

[11] Chintaman,Rout (2013)

[12] Id note11

affiliation are conferred equal rights at par with men in personal matters. Since rituals are inherent part of culture and religion so care must be taken to make the rights only uniform, keeping in view of the basic structure of the Constitution viz. secularism.

• *Alka Bharti (2013)*[13] also undertook a research study regarding *Uniform Civil Code in India- still a distant dream*. The objective of the paper was to discover the importance of Uniform Civil Code as a tool to create religious harmony, thereby promoting fraternity as enshrined in the Constitution of India. The scholar discussed the relevance of the fundamental rights and directive principle of states policy in the light of whether they are contradictory or otherwise.The scholar also discussed several court cases pertaining to the verdict of Apex in personal laws, setting a context for Uniform Civil Code. The study concluded with an observation that a strong political will is required along with the feeling of religious tolerance and mutual respect for each other.

• *V.R. Sai Sathya (2015)*[14] undertook a research study under *Constitutional history of India on Uniform Civil Code in India - An empirical study*. The objective of the study was to study the essentiality for India to construct a Uniform Civil Code for its citizens. The study concluded that the application of Uniform Civil Code

---

[13] Alka Bharti (2013)

[14] V.R. Sai Sathya (2015)

will lead to development of unity and integrity of nation as well as fraternity.

- *Asha Rani (2016)*[15] undertook a research study on "*A term paper on Uniform Civil Code*". The researcher examined the issue of Uniform Civil Code in historical perspective to explore why India need a Uniform Civil Code. The researcher was of the opinion that inspite of several Court verdict and societal interest, in favor of Uniform Civil Code, none could influence the legislatures who alone are empowered to make law. Also, enactment of Uniform Civil Code will ensure that no one can misuse religion and personal laws in the matter of exploitation of women and abridging their human rights. The study concluded with an observation that there is no necessary connection between religion and Personal Law in a civilized society. Marriage, divorce, adoption, succession, inheritance are matters of secular nature, and can, therefore, be regulated by law applicable to all persons in the country.

- *Personal Law Reforms and Gender Empowerment: A debate on Uniform Civil Code*, book by *Nandani Chavan and Jehan Kidwai*[16] is an attempt to study and discover the possibility of reforming Hindu as well as Muslim personal law from the women right perspective. The book deals with the study of personal

---

[15] Asha Rani,(2016)

[16] A debate on Uniform Civil Code, book by Nandani and Kidwai, hope india publication

law and debate on the need for Uniform Civil Code with special reference to gender justice.

- *Women and Social Reforms in Modern India: A Reader, a book* by *Sumit Sarkar and Tanika Sarkar*[17] is a study on on social reforms in women perspective. It discusses education and development of women of upper class as well as Muslim women in modern age with real life situation.

- *Lepakshi Rajpal and Mayank Vats (2017)*[18] undertook a research on *Uniform Civil Code and its legal dimensions*. The objective of the study was to analyse the concept of Uniform Civil Code and make people aware so that they can decide about the implementability in terms of its benefits for a better and just social order. The research methodology adopted was analytical and descriptive in nature, relying on secondary sources and class room discussion and lectures.The researchers studied three broad areas in their research i.e Uniform Civil Code and the Personal Laws, Secularism and the Uniform Civil Code and Uniform Civil Code and Gender Justice in the light of the fact that India is a highly divisive nation with numerous linguistic cultural and religious identities.The co-author concluded that there is no need for

---

[17]Women and Social Reforms in Modern India: A Reader, a book by Sumit Sarkar Tanika Sarkar Indiana university press 2008.

[18]Lepakshi Rajpal and Mayank Vats(2017)

codification of the Uniform Civil Code and the only need is to amend the Personal Laws.

- *Zoya Hassan and Ritu Menon (2005)* [19] conducted a *survey* research on Hindu and Muslim women, the findings indicated that as a group Hindu woman were stronger than Muslim women when compared on similar socio- economic background and regional location. However, insignificant variations were observed in matters of marriage, autonomy mobility and domestic violence. No apparent community based differences were observed in women's decision making, mobility and access to public places. The outcome of survey was that except poverty, religion did not influence per se the status of Muslim woman significantly. The researcher also found that poor socio-economic condition prevalent among Muslim women having marginal status get aggravated by their socially disadvantageous context.

- Recent anthropological studies have indicated that though Muslim men have more rights than women, but they are not frequently asserted. In a study at Chennai, researcher *Sylvia Vatuk* found that quite opposite to popular stereotype belief, unilateral divorce is rarely done whimsically. In order to escape legal obligation many men among Hindu and Christian just abandon their wives not going into the formalities of divorce. Similarly, Muslim male resorting to triple *talaq* attracts

---

[19] Zoya Hassan and Ritu Menon (2005)

social attention and find it difficult to get married again. In yet another study on middle class Hindu women in Delhi, researcher *Shreemati Basu* found that Hindu women rarely receive her due share of property despite of favorable inheritance law.

- Regarding the status of Bigamy in India the situation is that it is far more prevalent among Hindus than Muslims. As per last comprehensive survey[20] of 1971 indicate that about one crore Hindu male had more than one wife in comparison to 12 lakh Muslim male. However, recent National Family Health Survey of 2011, reveals that 1.7 % Hindu men and 2.1% of Christian men had more than one wife as compared to 2.5% of Muslim men. Polygamy in Muslim provides full protection of legal rights to second wife and children from her but among Hindus and Christian the second wife and her children have only a few enforceable legal rights. In-fact, the 2011 Census recorded a divorce rate of 2.3 (per thousand) with highest number amongst Buddhist, followed by Christians and then by Muslims.Overall scenario clearly indicate that legal reforms has not much impacted to improve the lives of women, therefore legal awareness and support network to access these rights is important. It also suggests that legal reforms must be accompanied by corresponding change in social value to avoid adverse effects, e.g ban on polygamy in Hindus leaves the second wife unprotected. The position of women has become vulnerable, after Apex Court verdict in 2010,

---

[20] comprehensive survey of 1971

while ignoring the established precedent in *D Veluswamy's* case, denied a woman right to claim maintenance in marriage like relationship.

- Legal author *R Maya and Rytim Vohra*[21] conducted a research study titled "*Empirical research on the need for Uniform Civil code in India*". The study having discussed various aspects of personal laws governing Indian society lamented that despite of active efforts by judiciary, it is the prime responsibility of the Union Parliament to enact Uniform Civil Code, but governments are often inclined towards political considerations and deterred by communal intolerance.

- National Political Party BJP had UCC in its 2014 election agenda, the party not only received a majority but also it was re-elected to power with a landslide victory in the 2019 elections, perhaps an endorsement by Indian voters. Today BJP and RSS are working together in this direction by citing the example of Goa, being the only state of the Union of India practicing Article 44, called Goa Civil Code, collectively known as Family Laws. The author [22] having selected a representative sample, conducted a survey amongst 100 people of age bracket 18 to 50 on two aspects firstly whether a common citizen of India is aware of different personal laws in India and secondly whether there is a need for enactment of Uniform Civil Code. The idea

---

[21] R Maya and Rytim Vohra, "Empirical research on the need for uniform civil code in India"

[22] Ibid note 21

behind the empirical research was to gauge the views and opinion of citizens of diverse background on basic issues relating to Uniform Civil Code. The study concluded with an observation that Uniform Civil Code is the need of the hour and government cannot use the excuse of communal backlash to delay it. If we wish to be a truly secular nation, as per preamble, then Uniform Civil Code cannot be denied to its citizens.

We must not forget that in an age of Globalization, of blurring of boundaries, of fusion of the wisdom of the east and west the development of Science and Technology has virtually converted the world into a potpourri. It has had helped in transcending the geographical boundaries, cultural context and ideological barriers. Different Personal Laws must have been a product of their own time. However, the large question in contemporary scenario is how far we have moved closer to the Constitutional commitment of a Uniform Civil Code as envisioned by the makers of the Constitution. Since still there is diversity of views on the issue of marriage, divorce, succession, inheritance and maintenance.

However, it cannot be denied and ignored that the personal laws in India are varied in their very source, philosophy and applicability. The major problem is of gathering people governed by different religious group on a common platform. Just like in most modern nation a Uniform Civil Code will strive to administer the same civil laws on all citizens, irrespective of their caste, religion or tribe. This can also be perceived by some as the denial of the right of the citizens to be governed by their choice of personal laws based on their religious affiliation or caste or tribe. There is also a need to study various personal laws in the light of their religious practices, tradition and custom for a better understanding.

Therefore, focus will be on how far the need for implementation of Uniform Civil Code is necessary in a fast globalizing world and what are the constraints involved? The following questions also need to be addressed in the debate on implementation of Uniform Civil Code.

- What can be the impact of socio-cultural ethos leading to Uniform Civil Code?
- How can Uniform Civil Code help in addressing the issue of discrimination against vulnerable groups and in its endeavor to harmonize different cultural practices?
- What are the legal aspects of Uniform Civil Code, vis-a-vis Various Personal Laws?
- What is the perception of society and outside world about Uniform Civil Code?
- Issue of Religious norms and family law: is it Normative Pluralism or Legal Pluralism?
- What is the role of Constitution as a unifying force in relation to Personal Laws?

Chapter I: Introduction

- What is the relevance of Uniform Civil Code in a democratic set up?
- What will be the impact of Uniform Civil Code on solidarity of nation and its fraternity?
- What is the role of Uniform Civil Code in bringing about Gender Equality? An attempt has been made to address these and many other such questions in the subsequent chapters.
- How long can Indian polity afford to hide behind vote bank politics? Perhaps now is the time for a study backed legislative mandate.

Chapter II
Historical Perspective of Uniform Civil Code

2.1 General:
Historically, India is known for both intrinsic unity as well as extrinsic plurality and diversity arising out of a number of forces such as religion, region, caste, creed, language, habitat, etc. Constitution of India promotes and protects intrinsic unity in diversity rich country. The partition of the country on the basis of religion has left deep rooted wounds, making the task of protecting its unity really challenging. India is a country with a rich cultural heritage, which has assimilated a vast variety of religions, cultures, traditions and languages within its fold. This is why, India is not only a country but a sub-continent as it stands out distinctly from the rest of the continent. This peculiar feature of India brings harmony among various political-social and religious faiths prevailing throughout its territory.

At the time of drafting of our Constitution word secularism was not inserted in the preamble but Article 25 to 30 of our Constitution provided the essence of secularism making it omnipresent. Thus, Part III of the

Constitution [23], comprising of fundamental rights, is woven around the idea of secularism. The term secularism was inserted in the preamble by 42nd Amendment[24], thereby making secularism as an integral part of the basic structure of the Constitution. The term secularism was inserted in order to counter the undercurrent of communalism and preventing any kind of confusion regarding secular nature of Indian Constitution. The Constitution guarantees to its citizens freedom of religion and conscience, and also restrains the state from making any discriminatory treatment on the basis of religion. One nation, one Constitution, one citizenship, one national anthem, are some of the salient features of Indian Constitution. The debate on Uniform Civil Code is always related with the issues of secularism and national integrity[25]. In legal Parlance, Uniform Civil Code stands for "administration of a set of civil laws to govern all people without any discrimination of religion". The common areas under Uniform Civil Code consist of marriage, divorce and adoption, inheritance. Lack of common code adversely affects the life of Muslim women.

India as a nation is known for land of cultural diversity, multiple languages, and religions. However, India as a nation has often faced numerous problems due to its different personal laws governing different communities

---

[23] Supra note 4

[24] Supra note 5

[25] Tahir Mahmood, personal Laws in Crisis, p.3(1986)

with distinct religion, custom, tradition and usage. The Constitution envisaged a Uniform Civil Code under Article 44, bringing in its ambit a large number of personal laws. However, despite of multiple challenges India has achieved a uniform legislation in almost every sphere of national life (civil, contractual, criminal etc.) except family and matrimonial laws. This is how an attempt was made in Article 44 to empower state with this responsibility. During Constitutional Assembly debate due to lack of consensus to arrive at a common ideology the Article was reduced to directive in nature rather than mandatory. The talk on Uniform Civil Code is going on since independence and from the time of the Constitutional Assembly Debates. The judiciary through various pronouncement has been playing a proactive role to enforce Uniform Civil Code. This has been critiqued as a Judicial overreach but by and large it has been appreciated by Indian masses of varied background as a positive sign. As Supreme Court has asked Union Government regarding its willingness to enact a Uniform Civil Code, in order to override age old inconsistent personal laws of different religious groups. Despite the heated debate on Uniform Civil Code one thing is undisputed and that is any provision of personal law that abridges or violate the fundamental rights stands Unconstitutional as per Article 13, in Part III of the Constitution[26] and so it must be struck down. Beside this inherent inconsistency in various personal laws has also

---

[26] supra note 4

been challenged on the grounds of Article 14, which guarantees the right to equality

2.2 Historical perspective:

It would be worthwhile to briefly study and look into the historical perspective of evolution of religious laws in India for a coherent and in depth understanding of the issue related to problem and challenges. Uniform Civil Code stands for a common code, applicable to all without taking into consideration their religion, race, caste, creed etc. At the present point of time it has posed a great challenge before India, that is, how to implement Uniform Civil Code. The makers of our Constitution willfully inserted Uniform Civil Code in the Part IV of the Constitution[27] that is directive principle of state policy and not in the Part III of the Constitution, comprising of Fundamental Rights. Under the Constitution of India in Part IV, Article 44, provides that the state shall endeavor to secure for its citizen a uniform civil code throughout the territory of India. Hindu legal history reveals that during the pre-independence era state did not interfere with Hindu law. The personal laws were regulating the affairs with complete immunity. State was interested only in social order and kept its hands off from the religious laws. Society was an organized unit at the time, with sages as Hindu leaders, who laid down certain universal laws. Social affairs were governed by these rules including religious ceremonies, rites and also acted as a

---

[27] supra note 1

code of ethics and morality. The socio-religious rules and civil laws were not separate. Hindu law was an integral part of the religion.

There is a common opinion regarding the fact that entire spectrum of socio – political – economic, life of the people was guided by divinely sages and philosophers, dominating the entire period. India being an ancient society was cohesive, leaving no room for conflict of personal laws and therefore the coexistence of various personal laws thrived.

In India, the evolution of Christianity finds its beginning with Saint Thomas Christians in Kerala in the 1st CE. This diversified into different churches as time went by. Later, several denominations were introduced with the advent of European missionaries and colonizers.

These denominations exist even today, they are primarily based on the form of Church governance. Thus, determining the authority for theology (Biblical interpretation), governance, worship, fellowship and ordinances. According to Protestants Christ invested this authority with the Bishops. Some examples of Protestant Christian Churches include; the Episcopal Church, Church of England (the Anglican Communion) believe this authority was invested by *Christ* in the Bishop and lay persons. The *United Methodist* Church in North America, *Lutherans* similarly invest this authority with Bishops. *Presbyterians* invest this authority with the elders and the *Pastors* jointly. *Congregationalist* invest this authority with local body of believers. However the denominations are based on several other factors and differences of beliefs such as the *Baptism* (gave rise to the *Baptists*, some of the *Pentecostal* Churches practice believer's *Baptism*), supernatural gifts (sign gifts, speaking of tongues, working of miracles, etc Protestants and Catholics believed these gifts to be given by Christ to the apostles to establish the Church and word of God), regional factors (such as nationality, language, society and politics). It is due to this regional factor that many of the state Churches such as *Anglicanism* of England, *Lutheran* of Germany continued to retain their regional identity even though being protestants, following a similar theology.

Christian personal laws do not find a clear mention in Christian religious texts. But the Christian Family law finds its genesis during the colonial times. In fact, during the British era the courts ruled that because Christian religion taught no personal law, the court had to examine a family's cultural habits[28]. These habits would help the court decide the personal law to be followed for its' judgement. However, with series of legislations and amendments since colonial era to today, the Christian personal law has found its shape in the form of a uniformly English law[29]. Today, in India provisions of Canon Law concerning marriage are recognized as personal law of Catholics in India. Christian marriages in India are regulated by Christian Marriage Act 1872.

---

[28] Abraham vs Abraham 1863

[29] Indian Succession Act 1865 - revised 1925, Divorce Act 1869

Inheritances are regulated via Indian Succession Act of 1925. An exception being the State of Goa, where Uniform Civil Code is in effect.

Jews in India are a non-singular community. They have made India their home at different points of time and location in history. Cochin Jews being the first to make the Indian subcontinent their home. Different Jewish communities thus went through a different cultural evolution thereby following set of sub-cultures within the religious community itself. Majorly of these Jewish communities are known by their primary place or residence or origin, such as *Bagdadi* Jews (Iraqi Jews), *Bene Israel*, *Cochin* Jews, *Ashkanazi* Jews, *Bnei Maneshi*, etc.

The Jewish personal laws are set according to customary ritual. Thus, even within Jews these laws can vary. The modern Jewish laws are an adaptation of *Mosaic* (*torah*) and *Talmund Law*. Lack of codification in regard to Jewish personal law is a matter of concern that has been highlighted by the court.

Zoroastrians, another minority community that found India their home in the Medieval Era. *Qisa-i-sanjan* (1599) holds the account of Parsi presence in the Indian subcontinent. The account was written in verse, a highly verbose style common to Persian poetry. These accounts though hold several different estimates of the year of migration.

Prior to 1837, Parsi's were by and large subject to common laws. Today, Parsi Marriage and Divorce Act

(1936) is dictated by the Special Marriage Act (1954) and inheritance is regulated by the Indian Succession Act of 1925 (with special provisions under Section 50 to 56 for Parsi intestate).

On the other hand, in the Islamic era, the Prophet was the religious leader for the Muslims who rose to the head of the state and it was only after his demise Islam followers found a problem of leadership. Consequently, Muslim leader selected *Abu-Bakr* as the first Imam or *Caliph*[30]. The *Caliph* was supposed to rule as the principle of holy *Quran*. No one could dare to challenge the authority of *Caliph* and change the law. However, Early-Medieval period around 11th Century witnessed the invasion of Indian peninsula by Muslim invaders. The most peculiar feature of invasion was subsequent settlement of Muslim rulers in India due to its absorbing and assimilating culture. This changed situation made it difficult for them to be governed by *Caliph* from a far-off distance. Thus, under the changed circumstances it became imperative for someone to resume the political leadership of Muslim community as a result of establishment of Muslim rule in India. These events finally led to the establishment of Muslim law in India as the law of the land and got enforced through the state apparatus. The rulers being of foreign origin neither accepted the Hindu law nor did they abolish the Hindu system of law rather kept it reserved for Hindus. Consequently, Muslims followed their system of law and Hindus were allowed to follow their

---

[30] Werner Menski, The Uniform Civil Code Debate in Indian Law: New Development and Changing Agenda (2008) 9(4) German Law Journal at 212-213

system of law during the period. This was a situation of two sets of personal laws existing parallel to each other simultaneously at that time.

The downfall of Medieval Empires in India around 17th century marked the beginning of British era in India. The Britishers realizing the multicultural character of Indian society with diverse systems didn't interfere with the Muslim law and judicial administration. They even went to grant legislative immunity to certain deeply interwoven religious issues of Hindu and Muslim law. However, subsequently Britishers changed the inhuman brutal criminal law of Mugal time by enforcing completely new criminal law. Britishers[31] chose not to interfere with the religious sentiments of Hindus and Muslims, in order to retain political stability. Therefore, the British while dealing with the religious and personal matters of both communities, adopted a stand of neutrality.

Thus, codification of laws dates back to colonial time. The legislative literature of India is being shaped by its colonial masters by playing an important role. In 1840, the Lex Loci Report [32], recommended the need for codification of Indian laws concerning crime, evidence, contract etc., but also recommended that the personal laws of Hindus as well as Muslim must be kept outside the codification process.

---

[31] Supra note 9
[32] supra note 2

Chapter II: Historical Perspective of Uniform Civil Code

It is well known that, in Islam the fountainhead of both Law and Religion is God. The basis of close relationship between *Shari'a* and *Fiqb*; that is the law conceived as the moral laws and the law conceived as the civil law. This is indicative of the fact that there is no clear distinction between law and religion in Islam. Moreover, we must not forget that Islam is a younger religion in comparison to the religious philosophy of Hinduism, Buddhism, Jainism and Christianity etc; who have matured and evolved over a comparatively longer period of time.

In 1780, Warren Hastings in Administration of Justice and Regulation made it clear that disputes arising out of family matters, must be governed by the respective personal laws of communities concerned as a policy declaration. Therefore, Britishers merely codified the law dealing with crime on secular line.

Today, there is a widespread misconception about the concept of divorce under Muslim law. No study can be complete unless we have a conceptual clarity and understanding of what we are talking about and what are the issues bothering our society having a direct bearing on the quality of our national character building. It is well known that Muslim marriage is a contractual marriage, where the separation or divorce also needs to fulfill certain conditions. This is an excellent provision of marriage providing a legal security at the very inception of marriage. In countries practicing common law system neither of the partner is empowered to give divorce of his own as in Islamic law, rather the power of granting divorce vests in the hands of Judiciary. Under the Islamic law countries, the right to divorce is put in the hands of man and women, depending on the type of separation.

Divorce by *talaq* is unilateral right of man in Islam but if he agrees to delegate and transfer his power of talaq, then under such circumstances the wife will also have the same rights known as (*Tafweedh-e-Nikah*). On the other hand (*Faskh-e-Nikah*) is the dissolution of marriage by an Islamic Court or Shariah council in UK, when the wife desire to proceed with divorce but the husband unreasonably refuses to grant talaq. According to Islamic jurist divorce is of only two type i.e *Bida* and *Soni*. *Bida* is innovative form of divorce as *talaq-e-biddat*, already declared unconstitutional by Supreme Court verdict in August/2017. Under the category of *Soni* which is by Prophet's order the divorce is of two kind i.e Revocable or irrevocable. Under revocable divorce a man after pronouncing talaq can return to his wife during seclusion (period of *iddat*) as in the case of *talaq-e-Ahsan* and *talaq-e-Hassan*. Under irrevocable divorce category comes *Khula* and *Mubarat* types of divorce. Khula is a procedure in which a woman can initiate divorce proceedings and can divorce her husband, by returning the dower (*mahr*) that she received from her husband while in *Mubarat* divorce is based on mutual dislike. This background regarding the scheme of divorce in Islam must be kept in mind for a fair and reasonable comparison with the provisions of divorce in other communities.

2.3 Initiative after independence:

With the independence of India in 1947, during the process of making of the Constitution of India, several rounds of debate and discussions were held in the Constituent Assembly on the notion of adopting Uniform Civil Code. Finally, personal laws were allowed to be retained for different communities. The members of the constituent assembly including then Prime Minister Nehru were of the view that in a nascent nation like India a certain amount of modernization is imperative before imposing Uniform Civil Code on citizens belonging to different communities, including Muslim.[33] Given the trying times of a transition of power, sensational partition and a nascent India, the framers of Constitution envisaged a Uniform Civil Code that would rest in the Directive Principles of State Policy as an embodiment of their wisdom only to be manifested when India would be ready to adopt it. Though leaders of that time were of the opinion to have a secular model on the pattern of western democracies. However, the outcome was a secular state with Liberty to have different personal laws for its different religious groups, which was much different than the secularism as practiced in the western world.

In this context it is very important to learn about what changes have taken place in our legal and political culture which went into the making of the Constitution? The

---

[33] Journal of Indian Law and Society Vol.5(Monsoon)JILS (2014)

wave of nationalism which began around the closing period of 18th century, reached its apex by the end of 19th century in the west.[34] This wave of nationalism entered India in the early part of 20th century and saw its expression in *Swaraj*, *Swadeshi* and *Quit India Movement* of Mahatma Gandhi, with a goal of involving masses in the struggle for independence. However, it was severally criticized by Tagore as it had it sway in the domestic politics of the country. He argued nationalism will preach specified territory for a nation, inhabited by people of one race, one language, one religion, one legal system with uniform laws applicable to all etc, in order to inculcate devotion and willingness to sacrifice anything and everything for the sake of the nation.

To substantiate Tagore, the immediate bitter experience of two world wars, taught us the danger inherent in the ideology of nationalism and that is why after the second world war nationalism became a hard concept being gradually replaced and relinquished in the era of globalization. But it is also a reality that various changes brought about by the concept of nationalism including the concept of law could not be changed overnight.

In contrast however, makers of the constitution were tasked to weave a homogenous constitution for a heterogeneous society, a society that at the time of independence was set in its mosaic frame and efforts were made to preserve its diverse nature. Yet, in a fast-paced

---

[34] ibid

changing, immigrating and globalizing era, it is but a melting pot. In the face of inevitability of a merging socio-cultural identity the task falls into the hands of today's legislature. Legislature is the voice of common man from the seat of democracy, several attempts to politicize this debate in election manifestos and campaigns have been made. Let us look further into the findings of expert bodies on the matter. Law commission of India in its fifteenth report,[35] mentioned that the perceptible combination of fundamental rights and religious dogmas practiced by all groups is the very founding stone of the Uniform Civil Code.

In order to avoid communal backlash, an awareness campaign is imperative for making the society more conscious and sensitive towards other communities in order to initiate a nationwide debate on UCC. This will act like a catalyst in realizing the objective of Uniform Civil Code. A man of ordinary prudence should find it just, fair and reasonable who has no religious bias or political consideration. The advantages of enactment and enforcement of a Uniform Civil Code are as under:

- National feeling of oneness and national integration will be enhanced.
- Litigation in personal law will decrease indicating better situation of gender justice.
- A comprehensive Code will avoid overlapping provisions of law thereby facilitating speedy justice.

---

[35] Law Commission of India, Fifteenth Report, 1960

- The true meaning of secularism will be realized in a democratic nation.
- The communal and divisive forces will be curbed down.
- Dream of One Nation One Code will be realized.

2.4 Conclusion:

Keeping in view of above discussion on historical background of UCC, it is worthwhile to mention that Goa Civil Code was enacted and enforced by the colonial rulers Portuguese during 19th and 20th century after several legislations. Goa became independent only in 1961 to be an integral part of India, so colonial laws were abolished, and central laws became operative in Goa. However, an exception was made to retain the family laws as they were accepted by all the communities residing in Goa. The most important provision in these family laws is regarding disposal of immovable and movable property in the event of death or divorce. The law provides both parents to have a common right over the estate and the property has to be divided equally. Son and daughter also have equal right on the property without any discrimination. The family law in Goa provides compulsory registration of marriage which helps in checking the social evil of child and bigamous marriage. To strengthen the family system which is the backbone of the society was the main philosophy behind the Goa Civil Code enacted by the erstwhile rulers of Goa. This also provided a spirit of tolerance between the couple and an inbuilt safeguard for protection against injustice. Former Chief Justice of India, Y. V.

Chandrachud regarding the dream of Uniform Civil Code for the the country, reiterated that its realization is found in Goa Civil Code and hopefully one day it will awaken the rest of the country.

The personal laws in India are inherently unequal since they are based on the practice of traditions of entirely different religions. Thus, retention of such different personal laws led to contradiction within the Constitution as a natural outcome. The very fact that Constitution recognizes existence of personal laws on one hand and on the other hand Article 44 expects that India to have a Uniform Civil Code at a later date, is the main bone of contention. This is coupled with the fact that Articles 14 to 19 of Indian Constitution which guarantees equal rights but in practice, divorce in Muslim law is entitled to a different treatment than Hindu law, consequently mere reading of Article 15 appears to make personal law unconstitutional. Not only this, Article 15 also requires non- discrimination on the grounds of sex, whereas Muslim personal law favors the men in many senses such as in the matter of extra-judicial divorce and polygamy. The right of equality before law could be interpreted as right of Muslim women to have four husbands. These issues remained unresolved in the Constitution and on top of it the irony is that awakened people of India including its political leadership either remained ignorant or unaware of it for a long time. Even various women's activist groups who demand and agitate for unequal treatment to women under the personal laws of Hindus as well as Muslims don't stress the need for Uniform Civil

Code, rather just call for equal rights in respective groups but refrain from calling the same law for all i.e. Uniform Civil Code.

Historically passing of Hindu Code Bill in 1950, was a turning point for all personal laws. The Hindu Code Bill aimed at bringing a series of legislation for secularizing the Hindu community by making law to suit the modern time, in essence abolition of old Hindu law, enactment of new law based on western lines for realizing equality of men and women, and other progressive ideas. The enactments and implementation of these laws also had impact on Muslim community. The Hindu Marriage Act of 1955 prohibited polygamy amongst Hindus and ensured the right of divorced wife for maintenance and alimony. This Act was applicable to everyone in India except Muslim, Parsis, Jews and Christians. Since Parsis and Jews form a very small minority, the Muslims only remained as a big community that is yet to be reformed on modern lines. However, there are several loopholes in the Hindu Act which leads to misuse of its provision thus it is very meaningful to develop a Uniform Civil Code for all religions in order to plug these loopholes. In the Indian legal system Uniform Civil Code can bring not only clarity but a better and just social order.

CHAPTER III
INTERNATIONAL PERSPECTIVE AND CURRENT TRENDS

3.1 International Scenario:

The very notion of Uniform Civil Code in European countries must have been influenced by similar code by the end of 19th century or in early part of 20th century with French Civil Code of 1804 in focus. It is interesting to know that, the French code was written on a clean slate, it abolished every pre-existing law and legal institution on its coming into force. This led to the replacement of all customary or statutory laws of different sections or class of people in one uniform law stated in the code. The other countries of Europe repeated this precedence in their respective codes.

In order to understand the legal pluralism along with problems and challenges related to Uniform Civil Code, we must appreciate that the very concept of uniformity is forced while that of Diversity is natural. According to

Hobbes[36] in a state of nature, people lived by their own group norms, which differ from group to group in one way or the other. Thus, Hobbes gave a vivid depiction of that society and conceived the idea of sovereign to whom all people expressed their allegiance in exchange for establishing an order. Austin[37] used that concept to define law in top-down terms that all law was direct or indirect command of the sovereign and whatever could not be proved so could not be law. Later on Jurist and legal philosopher like Hans Kelsen and Hart[38] gave a bottom-up description of all law by propounding that any norm or rule of conduct to be a law must be capable of being traced back to a *grundnorm* or rule of recognition, as a fundamental norm, order or rule that forms an underlying basis for a legal system . Therefore, to qualify to be a law it must be capable of being traced otherwise it is not a law. However, from 1930 onwards, many legal scholars including Ehrlich[39] started questioning the concept of law. The very basis of questioning was the difference between the state law and people's behavior noted by these scholars. In fact, people perceived and also practiced a lot of things which either have no connection with the state law or even if there was any connection, people behaved in such a flexible manner that they did not come in conflict with the state law. This is how over

---

[36] Austin, Hobbes, and Dicey, David Dyzenhaus-2011-Canadian Journal of Law and Jurisprudence 24(2):411-440

[37] ibid

[38] Kelsen,Hart,and legal normativity-Revues.org-openedition

[39] Eugen Ehrlich- Fundamental principles of the sociology of law, Transaction publishers New Brunswick (U.S.A.) and London (U.K) ,2009 google book

the years people have indulged in a lot of activities by forming clubs, religious groups, association or any other informal organization without coming in conflict with the state laws, even till date. In fact, the very norm set by these groups or bodies were such that they were highly respected as well as voluntarily accepted by all so that they could regulate large part of their lives without state intervention and at times even larger than regulated by the state laws. Therefore, customary laws find a place of prime importance in life of all societies. It was only with the establishment of state criminal laws were made uniformly applicable to all segments of society.

The above analysis brings us to a very important conclusion that legal centralism is a myth while legal pluralism is not only a reality but also the very essence of human life. Historically, Warren Hasting's regulation of 1772, can be called the first example of state recognition of legal pluralism[40]:

"In all suits regarding marriage, caste, and other religious usages and institutional law of the Koran with respect to the Mohammedans and of the Shastri with respect to the Gentoos shall be adhered to."

Everyone was governed by the state law aforementioned being an exception. This is a good example where the plurality of law was officially recognized in dominion India. These laws were administered in the same courts,

---

[40] Journal of Indian Law and Society Vol.5(Monsoon) JILS(2014)

but their distinct existence and operation was duly recognized and thus the regulation became a model for all European colonizers. However, prior to the advancement of the idea of nation state by Europe they conceived, pleaded and applied for a centrist's legal ideology in terms of unity of law. In fact, by then the scholars of legal pluralism recognized that in case of any conflict of state law with any customary or community law, it is the state law which would prevail, but if there is no such conflict the customary or community law can very well operate. We must remember that legal pluralism is an attribute of a social field and not of law or legal system. Legal pluralism is concomitant of social pluralism and refers to the normative heterogeneity leading to a dynamic condition. This conception of legal pluralism[41] fits very well with the social fabrics of India. As India is known for its tremendous diversity and social heterogeneity. Today all countries and societies are becoming more heterogeneous than ever before as a result of globalization and migration of a diverse population to common places across the world. Therefore, most countries including India are looking for solutions of such legal problems which are caused by social heterogeneity.

In this context *Salafis* are followers of Islam who advocate literal and to some extent binary interpretation of Islamic teachings. The invidious practice of triple *talaq* is confined to *Sunnis* alone, not only in India but

---

[41] M.B . Hooker, legal pluralism- An introduction to colonial and neither- colonial laws(1975)

worldwide. Although Pakistan and Iran are both Islamic countries, each has added or changed in some cases the laws regarding marriage and divorce as set out in holy text. It is often argued that religious minorities are relatively impervious to change. This is due to fear that any change in their practices might lead to a loss of their religious identity. But it's very interesting to note that this apprehension doesn't afflict the Muslims of Sri Lanka, where they form less than 10% of population. Sri Lanka's Marriage and divorce (Muslim) Act, 1951 as amended up to 2006 doesn't recognize instant divorce. Dr Mohammad Munir, prof of law and Director of Shariah Academy, International Islamic University Islamabad in his paper *"reforms in triple talaq in the personal laws of Muslim state and the Pakistani legal system continuity vs. change"*, rates the Lankan law as the *"most ideal legislation on triple talaq"*. In Pakistan a relook at triple *talaq* was initiated way back in 1955, when nationwide protest was held by the All Pakistani Women's Association. This demand prompted the Pakistan government to establish a seven member commission to probe into marriage and family laws. The commission came up with recommendations in 1956 that pronouncement of three *talaq* in one session should be counted as one. Thereby for a divorce to be effective the husband must have pronounced *talaq* in three successive *tuhrs*, and he could not divorce his wife till the time he secures an order to this effect from a matrimonial and family court. Later on when Bangladesh was born in the year 1971, the new nation inherited the law regulating marriage and divorce laws, consequently the triple *talaq* also remains abolished in Bangladesh as well. In comparison to the aforementioned neighboring countries surprisingly it took a long historical battle of litigation in India to realize the democratic right of Muslim women's i.e since Saha Bano time till recently when instantaneous form of Triple *Talaq* was declared unconstitutional.

With a globalizing world, fast changing social dynamics, world has become a melting pot. In the widely accepted contemporary social order and rule of law, it is a challenge for the states to protect interests of all communities specially when the community practices find itself in conflict with local laws or with one another, globalization has brought such inevitable bottlenecks to the shores. This marvel of heterogenous coexistence that has pooled individual talents from across countries, has also brought with them their unique cultures and values. Humans find themselves complying to law of host land but may be in violation with homeland laws, or vice versa. We shall make an attempt to understand the nature of complications that arise as a result of this cross-cultural migration and different family law setups in the host country and home country for individuals.The need for universal laws in family matters is also being felt in this age of globalization, it can be illustrated with the help of following examples[42]:

---

[42] Marriage and Divorce Law in Pakistan and Iran: The problem of recognition. Kristen Cherry, Tulsa Journal of comparative and International law 319(2010) volume 8/ issue 2, 9-1-2001.

Chapter III: International Perspective and Current Trends

In the first example, a newly wed Roshana left Iran with her husband to start a new life in the United States of America. However, soon after arrival the married life began to break down. This led her to receive divorce after a tedious court process. Relieved that she is now free from her husband, she made plans to visit her parents in Iran, only to discover that her divorce in US is not valid in Iran. She also learned that if she enters Iran, she would be returned to the control of her ex-husband's family and if she has remarried in US, her Ex-husband's family could accuse her of adultly and have her stoned. Here name has been changed to protect the identity.

The second example is of Hasan who married in Pakistan with a British women. After marriage they moved to the US, where differences crop up and Hasan divorced her according to the laws of his religion. Since the wife was a British national, the UK had never recognized this marriage. Even though she married again in England, the US never recognized the validity of their divorce. As far as Hasan is concerned he is still considered a married man back home, though to the rest of the world his status is either divorced or had never married. Here name has been changed to protect the identity.

There can be numerous such cases in the international arena as often marriages and divorce though legal in one country may not be recognized in another country for various reasons. These are often referred to as "Limping Marriages". We must remember that in this age of globalization where religious, cultural and social barriers are shrinking very fast and a new international community is on the verge of emergence. This brings us to a very serious question, what could be the model law governing marriage and divorce issues in international perspective so that it can have acceptance worldwide on the line of universal declaration of human rights? After all, to lead and live a happy and peaceful life in this age of inter-caste, inter-religious marriages or marriage between people of different nationalities, etc is nothing but an extension of basic human rights.

Clearly, efforts need to be made to ensure consistency of marital status across countries. Here the greatest challenge to overcome is a wide variety of religious and social ideas. So far in this connection two *Hague Conventions* have been held "*on recognition of divorces and legal separations*" to provide workable solutions. It is a multi-lateral treaty on private international law, which provides for the recognition of marriages. This convention was signed in 1978 by Luxembourg, Egypt and Portugal, later on by Australia, Netherlands and Finland. Since the outcome of these conventions is not a binding on the countries that may need it. (Ref 2) it is pertinent to mention herein that there is a need for marriage and divorce to conform to public policy, but whose? In this regard the public policy of Islamic countries differs amongst themselves, as do their laws. However, in today scenario, Pakistan and Iran as well as other members of the Islamic world are altering their laws especially on the issue of divorce and polygamy to adapt to the changing needs of their society.

3.2 Current scenario and media reports:

The paramount question is when innumerable legal codes flout the principal of equality before law then what prohibits the Indian Muslims from accepting a Universal Civil Code which endeavors to promote social equality and gender Justice. As Hindu and Muslim laws are not divinely ordained and are basically an outcome of Indian legal system which evolved during Britsh Raj. During 1955-56, Parliament passed a series of legislation with a view to reform legal practices governing Hindus during British Raj. Collectively known as Hindu Personal Law. During British Raj, Muslim Personal Laws were codified by the Central Legislature in 1937 with an objective of imposing uniformity throughout the British India. Parliament did not make any attempt to reform Muslim Personal Law in 1955-56 as it did with Hindu Personal Law because the then political leadership believed that Muslim minority, were traumatized post-partition and consequently should not be compelled, until the demand for reform comes from them voluntarily. However, this never happened to materialize, on the contrary even the reform process of Hindu Personal Law was delayed. Subsequently, many concessions were made, including retaining tax benefits for the Hindu Undivided Family (HUF) in order to bring about required legislation to be passed.

The post partition insecurity[43] can be attributed as a main cause of refusal of Muslims to adopt changes in their Personal law, however it got further aggravated when so called Hindu communal forces became the foremost proponents of Uniform Civil Code.

Most Hindus as well as Muslims are not aware of the fact that from 18th century onwards, British Judges decided cases pertaining to Muslims and Hindus based on their meagre understanding of Islamic and Hindu legal texts. This corpus of legal precedent came to be known as Anglo-Mohammedan Law and forms the basis of Muslim Personal Law. The irony is that even Muslim leadership refuse to recognize that precedents from classical period of Islam were nothing but products of their historical context and need not be valid across space and time. Prophet *Muhammad* was a social revolutionary and to understand his teachings it is *sine-qua-non* to differentiate between essential Islamic Principles and the historical circumstances in which they were applied. The important criteria is that the implementation of Islamic precepts must be sensitively related to changing times. Islamic teachings include two important socio-moral Principles of gender justice and social equality. It was Prophet who declared that women could inherit property and that a wife asset belonged solely to her. Not to mention it was the time when girl children were being buried alive at birth. All human beings are equal is the

---

[43] Ayoob Mohammed, *A just and equal code* article in daily The Hindu dated 21-5-2018

Chapter III: International Perspective and Current Trends

very essence of Holy *Koran*. This argument brings us to a very important conclusion that Muslim Indian should have no qualms about accepting a Universal Civil Code which promotes gender Justice and social equality and does not discriminate on the basis of religion or caste.

Besides this, it would be worthwhile to look at the recent media reports on the issue. It was in the daily news "The Times of India"[44] of dated 6 February 2018, that nobody has right to interfere if two adults get married: Supreme Court bench led by Chief Justice of India Dipak Mishra pronounced that no one, either individually or collectively, has the right to interfere in a marriage between two consenting adults. The bench also categorically declared the *Khap Panchayats* to refrain from playing the role of conscience keepers of society. As the Courts will go by law and not by tradition or gotra in order to ascertain the legality of a marriage.

In a similar development, it was also in the news whereby the All India Muslim Personal Law Board[45] asked grooms for oath against instant *talaq*. This is especially important in view of the verdict of Apex Court in declaring the practice of instantaneous triple *talaq* as unconstitutional with direction to the Union government to frame law on the subject to curb the menace of this arbitrary practice. Since the All India Muslim Personal Law Board

---

[44] The Times of India dated 6 February 2018.Dhananjay. mahapatra@timesgruop.com
[45] ibid

(AIMPLB) failed to convince the Supreme Court last year against banning instant triple *talaq*. Now they are all set to make it binding on Muslim men to commit in the *Nikahnama* (marriage contract in Islam) that they will not use the practice. This development in the Muslim personal law is a result of Muslim Women (Protection of Right on marriage) Bill making instant *talaq* a criminal act. All India Muslim Personal Law Board has drafted a model *Nikahnama*,[46] requiring the bridegroom to give an undertaking that he will not use instant triple *talaq* to divorce his wife. Its breach will be taken as invalid according to the *Shariah* or Muslim Personal law. The Bill to bring a new legislation for making the practice of instant divorce through 'triple *talaq*' among Muslims a punishable offense with 3-year imprisonment was pending for a long time but was finally passed and got the assent of the President of India despite the opposition by various lobby groups who opposed the Bill. The new legislation which makes the practice of instant divorce through 'triple *talaq*' among Muslims a punishable offense with 3-year imprisonment was challenged in the apex court as well as Delhi High Court. Both petitions were filed just a day after the assent of the President of India to this new legislation on the ground that the Muslim Women (Protection of Rights on Marriage) Act, 2019 is violative of the fundamental rights of Muslim husbands guaranteed under Article 14,15 and 21 of the Constitution and is liable to be struck down. There has

---

[46] Chandan Gowada article *Terms of separation* in The Hindu daily Friday, March 23, 2018

always been the history of appeasement and it has happened even at the time of Saha Bano Case of 1985. However, treating whimsical instant triple *talaq* as a form of mental cruelty on women it could have been taken care of by inserting an additional provision under section 498A of the Indian Penal Code to serve the purpose.

Indian society is a complex web of several types of life philosophy which guides the life of its several communities on the basis of cultural and religious beliefs. In this context the demand and move to recognise *Lingayat* as a separate religion must be seen in a political and historical context. Their request to be classified as a separate religion was turned down at the time of drafting of the Constitution of India. Though *Lingayat* were recorded as a caste within Hindu religion for the first time in the 1981 census done in Mysore state. It is in the light of such sensitive religious diversity the task of Uniform Civil Code has to be accomplished.

India as a nation is known for land of cultural diversity, multiple languages, and religions. Diversity is appreciated but India as a nation has often faced problems of integration and governance due to this, because different code governs, different communities coupled with different religions, customs, tradition and usage. The Constitution envisaged a Uniform Civil Code under Article 44, bringing in its ambit a large number of personal laws. However, despite of multiple challenges India has achieved a uniform legislation in almost every sphere of national life (civil, contractual, criminal etc.)

except family and matrimonial laws. This is how an attempt was made in Article 44 to empower state with this responsibility. During Constitutional Assembly Debate, due to lack of consensus to arrive at a common ideology the Article was reduced to directive in nature rather than mandatory. The talk on Uniform Civil Code is going on since independence and time of the Constitutional Assembly Debate. The judiciary through various pronouncement has been playing a proactive role to enforce Uniform Civil Code. There has been criticism of Judicial overreach but by an enlarge it has been appreciated by Indian masses of varied background, is a positive sign. As Supreme Court has asked Union Government regarding its willingness to enact a Uniform Civil Code, in order to override age old inconsistent personal laws of different religious groups. Despite the heated debate on Uniform Civil Code one thing is undisputed and that is any provision of personal law that abridges or violate the fundamental rights [47] stands unconstitutional as per Article 13, in Part III of the Constitution and so must be struck down. Beside this inherent inconsistency it has also been challenged on the grounds of violation of Article 14, which guarantees the Right to Equality.

Thus, there are several problems concerning Uniform Civil Code, such as the relation between secularism and Uniform Civil Code, different views on marriage, divorce and maintenance, how to integrate personal laws without

---

[47] Constitution of India part III Chapter on Fundamental Rights

hurting the religious sentiments of various stake holders, and need for codification, etc.

3.3 CONCLUSION:

The main controversy surrounding the Uniform Civil Code has been secularism and the freedom of religion guaranteed by the Constitution of India. India as a nation has no state-owned religion and state is not concerned with the relation of man with God. As a secular state it is only concerned with the relation between man and man and there is no room for discrimination on the ground of religion. Religion is only perceived as imparting the righteous way of life in Indian context; therefore, enactment of Uniform Civil Code is only possible by maintaining a delicate equilibrium between various personal laws, customs and common law governing Indian citizens. In order to understand this legal pluralism and problem and challenges related to Uniform Civil Code, we must appreciate the concept that *uniformity is forced while that of Diversity is natural.*

The above analysis brings us to a very important conclusion that legal centralism seems to be a myth while legal pluralism is not only a reality but also the very essence of human life. The notion of legal pluralism fits very well within the social fabrics of India. As India is known for its tremendous diversity and social heterogeneity. Today all countries and societies are becoming more heterogeneous than ever before as a result of globalization and movement of people of different backgrounds to a common place. Therefore, most countries including India are looking for solutions of such legal problems which are caused by social heterogeneity

Chapter IV
Legislative initiatives:

4.1 General

India being the largest progressive and evolving democracy of the world is blessed with a rich cultural heritage. A Culture that has tremendous potential to absorb and assimilate a vast variety of religions, cultures, traditions and languages. The Constitution of India is the supreme law of India. It frames fundamental political principles, procedures, practices, rights, powers, and duties of the government. It imparts constitutional supremacy and not parliamentary supremacy, as it is not created by the Parliament but, by a constituent assembly, and adopted by its people, with a declaration in its preamble. Parliament cannot override it.The partition of the country on the basis of religion has left deep rooted wounds, making the task of protecting its unity a challenge. At the time of drafting of Indian Constitution word secularism was not mentioned in the Preamble but Article 25 to 30 of Indian Constitution provided secularism in its essence. In particular, Part III of the Constitution comprising of Fundamental Rights is woven around the idea of secularism. However, the term secularism was inserted in the Preamble by 42nd Amendment Act, thereby making secularism an integral part of the basic structure of the Constitution. The term secularism [48] was inserted in order to counter the undercurrent of communalism and preventing any kind of confusion regarding secular nature of Indian Constitution. The Constitution guarantees to its citizens freedom of religion and conscience, it also restrains the state from making any discriminatory treatment on the basis of religion. One Nation, one Constitution, one Citizenship, one National Anthem are some of the salient features of Indian Constitution. It is very interesting to note that the debate surrounding Uniform Civil Code is always related with the issues of secularism and national integrity. In legal parlance, Uniform Civil Code stands for administration of a set of civil laws which govern all people without any discrimination of religion. The common areas under Uniform Civil Code comprises of marriage, divorce, adoption and inheritance. It is generally believed that lack of a common civil code in India has adversely affected the holistic integration of Indian Society and particularly the rights of women in certain sections of its society.

4.2 Constituent Assembly debates:

Personal laws were debated in the Constituent Assembly and an attempt was made to bring consensus in favor of

---

[48] supra note 6

Uniform Civil Code. The Constituent Assembly debated[49] under Article 35, regarding the issue of Uniform Civil Code. This debate generated a great deal of heat than light due to strong opposition by Muslim members. Mahmood Ismail from Madras advocated that right to stick to one's own personal law and religion comes under fundamental rights. After independence, the issues of personal laws and Uniform Civil Code were clouded by politics of appeasement and vested interest at national and regional level. It was also mentioned that personal laws were a part of the way of life of a particular community and part and parcel of culture and religion. Therefore, any interference with personal laws would amount to interference with the way of life of those who have been observing these from generation to generation. It was also elucidated that religious and cultural ethos of the people must not be hindered by an emerging secular state of India.

Mahboob Ali Beg[50] was of the view that civil code incorporated in Article 35 doesn't include family law and inheritance law. In fact he advocated inserting a proviso to keep the matters related with personal law out of it. He went further in claiming that the very concept of Uniform Civil Code clashed with the religious and cultural freedom guaranteed in the Constitution. He was apprehensive that the state may violate the religious

---

[49] Constituent Assembly Debates, Volume VII, NOV- 23-1948

[50] M.A.Beg Sahib Bahadur's Speech in the Constituent Assembly,Constituent Assembly Debate,Vol.VII(1949),p.542-543

freedom of its citizens under Article 35. He made a note of caution in following words:

"What the British in 175 years failed to do or were afraid of doing. What the Muslims in the course of 500 years refrained from doing, we should not give power to the state to do at all once...I submit Sir, that we should proceed not in haste but with caution, with experience, with statesmanship and with sympathy."

Reacting on the above antagonistic attitude the people members of Hindu community, holding protagonist attitude, expressed contrary view. K.M Munshi [51] expressed the following:

- Even without Article 35, Union Parliament is empowered to enact a Uniform Civil Code, as the Article guaranteeing religious freedom, empowers the state to regulate secular activities related with religion.
- In some very old Muslim countries, such as Turkey and Egypt, personal laws of religious minorities were not protected.
- Certain Muslim communities such as *Khojas* and *Memons* did not want to follow *Shariat* but were compelled to do so under the Shariat Act, 1937.
- European Countries have uniform laws applied to even minorities.

---

[51] Id note 39

Chapter IV: Legislative Initiatives

- Religion should be divorced from personal law. The Hindu Code Bill did not confirm in its provisions to the precepts of Manu and Yajunavalkya.
- Personal laws discriminated between person and person on the basis of sex which was not permitted by the Constitution.
- People should outgrow the notion given by British that personal law was a part of religion.

To quote in the words of K.M Munshi[52], "*I want my Muslim friends to realize that the sooner we forgot this isolationist outlook of life, it will be better for the country. Religion must be restricted to sphere which legitimately appertain to region and the rest of life must be regulated, unified and modified in such a manner that we may evolve, as early as possible, into a strong and consolidated nation.*" Being a member of Constituent Assembly while speaking on Muslim law reforms he mentioned about the examples of Turkey and other Muslim countries of the Arab world and Middle East. The Muslim members took a strong opposition to it and mentioned that Muslim world are not uniform, and India never sided with Turkey on this issue, moreover there are several other Muslim countries in the world who have also not changed their *sharia* law on the issue in debate. It is also important to note that unlike other religions, *Quran* contains a complete code of law. Therefore, it can only be changed as per the procedure laid down in that law and any attempt from outside to bring about a change

---

[52] Constituent Assembly Debates, Volume VII, NOV- 23-1948

in Muslim law can be unconstitutional if Muslims are not taken into confidence prior to such a change.

The efforts made by Dr. Ambedkar are worthwhile to mention here, he called upon the Muslim members "*Not to read too much into Article 44, even if Uniform Civil Code is brought into force it would be applicable on those who would consent to it.*"

The scenario was different in post independent India as the issue of personal laws got politicised. The Constituent Assembly got trapped in a heated debate on the issue of Uniform Civil Code. In fact, the debate on Uniform Civil Code divided the House on communal lines. Muslim members opposed it while Hindu members supported it.

Mohammad Ismail[53] of Madras cited precedent of former Yugoslavia where, three distinct communities of Serbs, Croats and Bosnian were living together, and Bosnian Muslims were allowed to have their own personal laws. However, today Bosnia and Herzegovina stand out as an independent Nation from 3 March 1992, being a break away part of former Socialist Federal Republic of Yugoslavia comprising of Republics of Bosnia, Macedonia, Serbia, Croatia, Montenegro and Slovenia. This split was a result of ethnic conflict. The disintegration of Yugoslavia occurred due to political upheavals and conflicts after the death of longtime Yugoslav leader Josip bronze Tito in 1980. The

---

[53] Constituent Assembly Debates, Volume VII, NOV- 23-1948

Chapter IV: Legislative Initiatives

Yugoslavia split in the early 1990s was on account of the unresolved issues which triggered a bitter inter-ethnic war in the east European part, resulting in creation of seven different countries. The author had the opportunity to work as a Human Right officer during 1999-2000 as a member of International Police Task Force of United Nation Mission in Bosnia and Herzegovina. During the UN mission on the basis interaction with different ethnic groups of Bosnian, Serbs and Croats while dealing with civil and local Police and Civil Administration issues on a routine basis, the author felt that among other causes lack of homogeneity in personal laws might have compounded as one of the causes of disintegration of the former Republic of Yugoslavia.

However, in the Indian context after enactment of Hindu Code the demand for reforms in Muslim Code and demand for Uniform Civil Code gained substantial momentum. As a result of it, all laws including personal laws are subject to change or amendment by Parliament or Legislature. As far as the recognition of personal laws is concerned, the Constitution of India does recognize their validity and continuance, Entry 5 of List III of 7th Schedule read with Article 372.

Legislative reforms in Hindu and Christian laws have paved the way for reforms in other religious personal laws particularly Muslim laws. It has created a movement to bring about a greater degree of uniformity among different personal laws in India. Today a lot of debate is going on within various communities to reform, particularly concerted efforts are being made in the field of family laws to reform from within. Socio-legal studies suggest that socio-economic factors are correlated with gender equality within the family set up rather than religious law. However, domestic violence as an emerging key area of family law has cut across community identities and larger concerns. At the time of colonial rule, personal laws were determined by the faith and they governed the affairs concerning marriage and inheritance. Although British in India followed the precedent of Mughal rulers in the matter of personal laws. It is also claimed that these personal laws were being administered by a secular judiciary instead of religious group. This situation led to a transformation of Hindu and Islamic laws as a result of passing through a process of translation, interpretation and adjudication by British Judges and came to be known as Anglo-Hindu and Anglo-Mohammedan laws.

4.3 Legislative efforts after Constitution came into force:

On 26 of January 1950, Constitution of India came into force. Under Article 44, it provided that state shall endeavor to establish a Uniform Civil Code [54] for its citizens throughout the territory of India. Two prominent schools of thought that supported Uniform Civil Code were liberal nationalist like Minoo Masani, who believed that community based personal laws will be a threat to national consolidation. On the other hand women leaders

---

[54] supra note 1

Chapter IV: Legislative Initiatives

at that time such as Hansa Mehta and Amrit Kaur perceived personal laws to greatly disadvantage the position of women in India. The irony was that demand for Uniform Civil Code was not only opposed by minorities but also by a significant section of conservative Hindus, viewing this as unwanted interference by the state in the religious matters. The agenda of the political battle of the period centered around debates on Hindu law reform instead of intervention in all personal laws in general. The victory in the general election of 1952 provided the then government an opportunity to enact the Hindu Codes. It is worthwhile to mention herein that before new Hindu Code, Hindu law was far behind Muslim Personal law in terms of women rights, as Muslim women could hold and inherit property, their consent was necessary for marriage, could act as guardian of minor and last but not the least, after the reforms of 1938, muslim women could also initiate a divorce.

Besides Hindu Code, legislative initiatives include introduction of a voluntary Uniform Civil Code i.e the Special Marriage Act of 1954. This Act was basically meant to facilitate inter-religious marriages, with the person married under the Act to be governed by Indian Succession Act, of 1925 for divorce, maintenance and succession. Thus, Special Marriage Act provided greater equality between men and women.

The personal laws governing religious groups is the oldest part of legal systems in India. The brief of various legislations related to personal matters enacted by the Parliament of India after independence are summarized as under:

- <u>The Special Marriage Act, 1954</u>[55]: It provides for a special type of marriage in certain cases, for their registration and divorce. The Act provides for solemnization of marriages by registration not only to Hindus but to non-Hindus, as well as foreigners marrying in India, who do not want to perform ceremonial marriage under their respective personal laws.
- <u>The Hindu Marriage Act, 1955</u>[56]: It is an Act which amends and codifies the laws concerning Hindu marriages and is applicable to majority population of Hindus. Though, registration is optional under the Act, but ceremonial marriage is essential. The legal issues of divorce and maintenance are being taken care by this Act.
- <u>The Hindu Succession Act, 1956</u>[57]: It is an Act governing legal issues related to succession among Hindus.
- <u>The Hindu Minority and Guardianship Act, 1956 and Hindu Adoption and Maintenance Act, 1956</u>[58]: These Acts deal with the law related to succession, adoption and maintenance among Hindus.

---

[55] <u>The Special Marriage Act, 1954</u>

[56] <u>The Hindu Marriage Act, 1955</u>

[57] <u>The Hindu Succession Act,1956</u>

[58] <u>The Hindu Minority and Guardianship Act, 1956 and Hindu Adoptation and Maintenance Act,1956</u>

Chapter IV: Legislative Initiatives

- **The Parsi Marriage and Divorce Act, 1936**[59]: The Act was amended in 1988 to deal with law relating to marriage and divorce among the Parsis in India.
- **The Indian Christian Marriage Act, 1872**[60]: It was enacted on 18th day of July 1872 to consolidate and amend the law related to the solemnization of Christian marriages in India.
- **Other important legal provisions**: The Muslims in India are governed by The Muslim Women (Protection of Rights on Divorce) Act 1986, The Muslim Women (Protection of Rights on Divorce) Rules 1986, The Muslim Personal Law (Shariat) Application Act 1937, and The Dissolution of Muslim Marriages Act 1939.

A great deal of debate pertaining to community identity and role of state was stirred in modern India during the Saha Bano Case of 1985. In this landmark Judgement the Apex Court held that Saha Bano Begam, a 60-year-old divorced Muslim woman had a right to claim maintenance from her former husband under Section 125 of the Criminal Procedure Code. It was a bold Judgement in favor of vulnerable class of Muslim women who were victims of injustice of practice of instantaneous talaq. However, the timings and observation on Muslim law by the Judges led to a growing clamor by All India Muslim Personal Law Board (AIMPLB). In the face of a growing discontentment among conservative Muslim section, the then government on a narrow political line to placate the

---

[59] The Parsi Marriage and Divorce Act,1936

[60] The Indian Christian Marriage Act,1872

situation decided to contain conservative opinion by enacting what came to be known as Muslim Women (Protection of Rights on Divorce) Act, 1986. The enactment of this Act effectively nullified the spirit of the Saha Bano verdict as it's legislated position in Muslim law now required the husband to only make "a fair and reasonable provision" for providing maintenance during the *Iddat* period of three months after divorce. The Act, 1986 was perceived not only discriminatory towards Muslim women but also appeasement of Muslim men by Hindu nationalist as well as by liberals. Thus, the core issue of maintenance enjoyed by other Indian women was denied to Muslim women. It was also perceived as a step not in the direction of Uniform Civil Code but against the Uniform Civil Code. Later on, during 1999 to 2004 BJP led coalition government of NDA at the centre also did not take any step in the direction of Uniform Civil Code.

However, over a period of two decades, due to determination of Muslim women for their just right, the Muslim Women[61] (Protection of Rights on Divorce) Act, 1986 has been interpreted by Judiciary to hold that the quantum of "reasonable and fair" provision during the *Iddat* period had to be sufficient to maintain the divorced woman for remaining part of her life.

---

[61] Muslim Women (Protection of Rights on Divorce) Act, 1986

4.4 Recent initiatives in the direction:

The election manifesto of BJP during 2014, general election says:
"Article 44 of the Constitution of India lists Uniform Civil Code as one of the Directive Principle of State Policy. BJP believes that there cannot be gender equality till such time India adopts a Uniform Civil Code, which protects the rights of all women, and BJP reiterates its stand to draft a Uniform Civil Code, drawing upon the best traditions and harmonizing them with the modern times."

However, after a period of three decades of weak coalition governments at centre, this time BJP had a landslide majority in Parliament. But it is yet to be seen in action in relation to the commitment of Uniform Civil Code. This is because equality of women was the key issue for some of our women members in Constituent Assembly to get Article 44 embodied in the Constitution of India. It can be inferred from the Constitutional debates that in their mind the plight of Hindu women was more significant than the plight of Muslim women. At that time the multiplicity of Hindu Law was creating inequality of women, particularly in property issues. Despite a series of legislation on women rights, much relief has not been secured to women. A lot still needs to be done for socio-economic empowerment of women so that they can take advantage of laws ensuring equality to them.

However in recent times, Hon'ble Supreme Court has pronounced judgements pertaining to society at large i.e on 22-Aug-2017, in the Case of triple *talaq* or *talaq-e-biddat* or Instantaneous *talaq*[62], Hon'ble Apex court in this case held that this practice is arbitrary as marriage can be broken whimsically without any attempt at reconciliation. Thereby, declaring it unlawful and unconstitutional. However, the theory of *one nation and one code* has several challenges to come across. It creates a situation where Constitution and religious laws seem to clash. Though, believers of a particular religion are free to keep their customs, but a dispute before the court of law in India should be settled on the basis of a common law. The code of a nation must prescribe to all people equal rights and obligations and allow no discrimination or even special rights on the basis of religion, caste, gender or sex. This will pave the way for not only real freedom of religion to an individual but also fulfill constitutional aim of a long awaited Uniform Civil Code. It is an irony that, as long as religion-based laws will remain in operation, the conflict will remain unresolved and clergy will always accuse the court of interference whenever court deliver a verdict not be acceptable to them.

The issue of anomalies in maintenance granted to Muslim Women was brought to the knowledge of Hon'ble Apex Court by Danial Latif, Advocate of Saha Bano's Case of 2001. It was held by the Court that the provisions of the Muslim women[63] (Protection of Rights on Divorce) Act,

---

[62] Shayara Bano and others vs Union of India and ors, WP(C) No.118/2016 SC
[63] supra note 50

1986 must be read in conjunction with the Right to Equality and Right to Live with Dignity and directed that the lump sum amount granted to a divorced Muslim women must be sufficient to maintain for her life time. Thus, for some time Muslim women enjoyed better claims for maintenance than other women till the upper limit in Criminal Procedure Code was revised.

Since 1980, Courts are continuously pondering on the question of Islamic law and have delivered interpretation to favor oppressed women, however it has invited a minimal resistance from Muslim leaders in a fast modernizing India. In yet, another important case of Shamin Ara (2002), the Court verdict was that a husband did not have a unilateral right of triple *talaq*, but it must be well reasoned one for divorce with attempts of reconciliation, rather than whimsically uttering three *talaq* times.

As a consequence of divergent views among Muslim Community over a period of time since independence, the Daniel Latif and Shamin Ara decisions did not evoke much protest. The scope of Muslim Personal Law has also been broadened over a period of time and different Muslim voices have come forward to assert their individual identities and views on issues of diverse social interest. All India Muslim Personal Law Board was founded in 1973, and it has emerged as the main representation on various issues and questions related to Muslim Personal Law. It has acquired the status of pleading in various Court cases and being in consultation with the government.

Over the years, All India Muslim Personal Law Board has been a source of intense criticism due to its domination by Hanafi Sunni Ulama from *Darul Uloom Deoband*, a centre of Islamic learning. It was pointed out by eminent historians of Indian *Shiasm*, Professor Justin Jones[64], that this perceived domination led to the creation of the All India Shia Personal Law Board and All India Muslim Women Personal Law Board. This led to resignation of many important *Barelvi* scholars from the All India Muslim Personal Law Board.

The emergence of alternative vision on Muslim Personal law is an outcome of these bodies who have challenged the authority of All India Muslim Personal Law Board by speaking on behalf of Indian Muslims. Noted political thinker Narendra Subhramaniam is of the opinion that, the divergence of opinion over the issue of instantaneous and unilateral triple *talaq* prevented the All India Muslim Personal Law Board from becoming a party in the famous Shamim Ara Case at the Supreme Court.

Meanwhile, the establishment of All India Muslim Women's Personal Law Board and rapidly grown Muslim Women Non-Government Organizations like *Awaaz-e-Niswan* (Mumbai) are busy spreading legal awareness.

---

[64] Jones, Justin(ed) 2015, *The Shi'a in Modern South Asia: Religion, History and Politics, Cambridge University Press, India*

Chapter IV: Legislative Initiatives

They are championing the cause of Muslim women's rights through Islamic scripture and appropriate interpretation of Sharia. This situation coupled with the spread of literacy, awakening and role of media is causing fragmentation of orthodox religious authorities and at the same time new groups are emerging to question religious orthodoxies. Among all these activities, the most powerful tool to readdress the grievances of Muslim women is none other than the Women Muslim groups. As besides advocating and creating legal awareness, they are assisting women in distress with their daily interaction with law, i.e, ensuring maintenance issues, secure custody rights or guarding women against domestic violence.

Starting of Muslim Women's Sharia Courts led by female Islamic Scholars in the States of Maharashtra, Odissa, West Bengal and Tamil Nadu, is an initiative of Bhartiya Muslim Mahila Andolan, is yet another step in ameliorating the situation of Indian Muslim women. They help in facilitating aggrieved women to claim Justice as a Muslim women by maintaining a delicate balance between choice for Muslim women between enjoying their right to equality as a woman and their right to their religion as a Muslim.

The socio-religious scenario in India is undergoing a fast transformation as sweeping legislative reforms in Hindu, Christian and Parsi laws are being accompanied by drastic changes witnessed in Muslim law over a few decades. In this connection it is worthwhile to understand that the Hindu Code reforms of 1955-56, didn't bring position of equality between Hindu men and women. It happened only after 2005 Amendment[65] in the Hindu Succession Act that the daughters could have a share of Hindu joint family property and got the right for its partition as a manager. The agricultural land was also brought under the purview of the Hindu Succession Act in 2005. Interestingly, the reforms in Hindu Law during 1955-56, which empowered Hindu women a right to inherit property, did not apply to agricultural land for almost five decades, despite the fact that agriculture land is the most valuable and prevalent form of property acquired by a family in India.

Today, the scenario has changed. Even tribal women who were denied the benefits of reforms in Hindu Law have begun to challenge their rights in Court. It is very interesting to know that in the year 2013, a group of Tribal women from *Kinnaur* district of *Himachal Pradesh* have challenged the constitutionality of old colonial law which recognized the customary practice of denying tribal women from inheriting ancestral property. Earlier, Oran and Ho communities of Jharkhand had also challenged the Constitutionality of the Land Tenancy Act of *Chotanagpur*, as the Act was discriminatory by allowing only male descendants to cultivate forest land. Illogical apprehensions were raised by Government officials as well as Tribal leaders by arguing that if tribal women are allowed inheritance it might lead to the

---

[65] The Hindu Succession (Amendment) Act, 2005

alienation of tribal land to non-tribal persons. The Apex Court in the Danial Latifi Case,[66] although upheld the constitutionality of the Act but made an important observation that it had to be interpreted while keeping in mind the Constitutional Right of life and livelihood. Thus, while upholding the male rights to succession, it was held that female heirs of last male tenant could hold and use the land in case of their dependency for livelihood on it. This is how Apex Court by a just and harmonious interpretation of statute provided a reasoned economic solution to tribal women without nullifying the tribal laws.

Many aspects of Christian Personal Law were also harmonized by Judicial pronouncement. The Apex Court in another landmark case of Mary Roy's[67] in 1986, held that the provisions of the Travancore Syrian Christian Act of 1916, and Cochin Succession Act of 1921, were unconstitutional as they arbitrarily infringed the right of Syrian Christian women on their paternal property. But Mary Roy had to wait till 2010 when the decree in this case was executed and she could get back her share of her father's property from her brother.

Another important matter came up before Supreme Court which related to provisions of Section 118 of the Indian Succession Act, which was drawn from English law and clearly laid down the condition that no Indian Christian

---

[66] Danial Latifiand ANR Vs. Union of India, 2001

[67] Mary Roy v. The State of Kerala 1986 AIR 1011, SCR (1) 371

with living relatives could surrender his property for religious and charitable purposes unless provided by a will a year before death. This clause was inserted to prevent death bed bequests, often made under the influence of a priest. In 2003, the Apex Court, while rejecting Father Vallamattom's[68] claim of right to make religious bequests was protected under the right to practice one's religion as there was nothing to show that the disposition of property for religious purposes was integral to Christianity. The Court held that it was violative of Article 14 of the Constitution and hence, unconstitutional. It was only recently that law of divorce for Indian Christian women was overruled. The law treated women as property by allowing husband to claim monetary damages to claim in case of adultery. The Court had the power to decide property of an adulterous women on her children on divorce, but an adulterous man had no such liability. Till 2001, a Christian woman could not claim more than 20% of her husband's income as alimony. -Provisions for maintenance under the Christian law are contained in The Indian Divorce Act 1869 which was amended in 2001. Thus, socio-religious reforms in this direction were carried out by National Democratic Alliance Government during (1999 to 2004), a backed up by a wide acceptance from Churches and Christian groups as a result of deep process of consultation before with the respective stake holders and interest groups. At present, the scenario is much better than a decade before, as development among Hindu, Muslim and Christian

---

[68] John Vallamattom's and ANR vs Unions of India (2003)

community shows symptoms of a greater congruence despite the different personal laws. However, these efforts are directed towards Uniform Civil Code. In the series of ongoing efforts Dr Justice B.S. Chauhan former Judge Supreme Court of India and Chairman Law Commission of India [69] made an appeal on dated 7th October 2016 by throwing a questionnaire containing, 16 question with multiple choice and brief narrative in the public domain for eliciting the response of people on family Laws and Universal Civil Code. The questions are based on awareness about the Constitutional provision of Universal Civil Code and what all should be included from the Personal Laws of all religion in the U.C.C. i.e Marriage, Divorce, Adoption, Guardianship and Child Custody, Maintenance, Succession and Inheritance, etc? The effort aims at soliciting opinions and ideas of people of all walks of life about the modalities of initiating the family law reforms in a cohesive manner without compromising the plurality and diversity of Indian society. Law Commission of India [70] received an overwhelming response of more than 40,000 people within the deadline of 45 days. However, the All Indian Muslim Personal Law Board (AIMPLB) criticized the initiative of the Law Commission of India by commenting that it was uncalled for. This was probably because one of the sensitive questions in the questionnaire was should the triple *talaq* be abolished and whether U.C.C. should be optional? The objective of the

---

[69] Appeal by Chairman Law Commission of India dated 7, October 2016

[70] supra note 58

Commission was to address the issue of discrimination against the vulnerable groups and endeavor to harmonize different cultural practices.

4.5 New frontiers of Legislative reform:

Personal laws only govern a few issues of marriage and inheritance. Interestingly, new family laws are focusing at common family experience shared by all women with an objective of ameliorating and improving the situation of women irrespective of religious laws. In this direction most valuable intervention by State has been the enactment of Domestic Violence Act [71] of 2005, for protecting women from abuse within family set up. The Act protects and covers all women in household setting including an unmarried female partner. Under the Act, definition of violence besides physical also take into account verbal, economic and emotional violence. The Act further guarantees to secure shelter to women, giving them right to reside in their matrimonial home irrespective of right or title to it. The courts are also empowered to pass varied case specific protection order to safeguard women.

There is a growing realization that the contribution of a married woman to family is immense and it cannot be quantified in economic terms. Studies have revealed that as a consequence of divorce or widowhood, it is the woman who suffers a great deal of economic loss. There

---

[71] Domestic Violence Act, 2005

are numerous cases pending in various courts, where it is very difficult to secure maintenance order as a result of husband disposing of property, leaving job, or not disclosing assets to prove that he is unable to maintain his wife. Maintenance under the law is not a property right and it stops if women remarries, is gainfully employed or dies. Perhaps the greatest challenge here is that the non-financial contribution of a woman in rearing family and to facilitate her husband to accumulate property is not addressed anywhere. Studies reveal that the most important hardship a divorced woman come across among different religious communities is the loss of a safe shelter as the title conventionally belongs to either her husband or her in-laws.

Realizing this practical aspect, legislators are working on creating a separate property regime for married couples. Right to matrimonial property is recognized in the Civil Code of Goa, since 19th century and it needs to be followed by other States. Legislature in Maharashtra is considering a Bill which will award half of the husband's property to a married woman. The Central Marriage Laws (Amendment) Bill of 2010, having been approved by the Union Cabinet intends to amend Hindu Marriage Act and Special Marriage Act to enact provisions to empower divorced wife to claim half the share of her husband's residential property. The irony is that the opposition for such social legislation does not come from minority groups but comes from strong male groups like "Save the Indian Family Foundation" who without evidence, seek to defend men's 'interest', argue that laws in India favor women. Meanwhile, courts are trying to quantify the contribution of women as a homemaker. The Apex Court in Lata Wadia's Case of 2001 held ₹ 3500 as a national monthly income of a homemaker in small town in India.

The question of solemnizing a second marriage by a Hindu husband by adopting Islam was discussed in famous case of Sarla Mudgal v. Union of India. The Court was of the view that it would amount to abuse of personal laws. It was held that such an act would amount to an offense under Section 494(5) of Indian Penal Code 1960 because Hindu marriage can only be dissolved under Hindu Marriage Act,1955 and by embracing Islam and marrying again does not dissolve the marriage under Hindu Law. The Judiciary was of a strong opinion that it is high time for a Uniform Civil Code to be introduced and Article 44 to be taken out of cold- store. The Court went further by stating that where more than 80% citizens have been brought under codified personal law, now there is no justification to keep in abeyance, the Uniform Civil Code for all the citizens in the territory of India.

Yet another important verdict which called for the implementation of Uniform Civil Code was a case involving a priest Mr. John Vallamatton of Kerala[72], who challenged the Constitutional validity of Section 118 of Indian Succession Act. This Act was applicable for non-Hindus in India. The contention raised by the Appellant was that Section 118 is discriminatory as it imposes unreasonable restrictions on Christians for donation of

---

[72] supra note 57

Chapter IV: Legislative Initiatives

their property for religious or charitable purposes by way of will. The full bench having heard the averments of Petitioner and Union struck down the section as unconstitutional and directed the Union Parliament to take concrete measures to enact Uniform Civil Code. It was also reiterated that by removing inherent contradictions based on ideologies in personal laws, a common civil code will emerge to help the cause of national integration.

From Judicial point of view, the Directive Principles of State Policy[73] are not enforceable in Court of law but these principles are fundamental in the governance of the country and it is the duty of the State to apply these principles in making laws. However, Courts are of the view that though Directive Principle are not justiciable, but they are as much part of the Constitution as the Fundamental Rights and hence deserve as the attention and importance as the Fundamental Rights draw. The Court also held that the Fundamental Rights enshrined in Part III of the Constitution must be harmonised with the Directive Principles enshrined in Part IV of the Constitution and such harmony is the basic structure of the Constitution. This will be equally applicable in the enactment of a Uniform Civil Code, enumerated in Article 44 of the Constitution. After the Indian independence in 1947, the main problem and challenge before the Constituent Assembly was drafting of a new Constitution and its subsequent smooth enforcement

---

[73] The Constitution of India part IV

keeping the objective of unity of the nation at the forefront. The makers of the Constitution deliberately left the enactment of Uniform Civil Code as a piece of future Legislation at appropriate time and after 70 yrs of independence it is perhaps one of the biggest problems as well as a great challenge before Indian Legislature.

In this connection it is interesting to learn that Goa Civil Code was enacted and enforced by the Portuguese during 19th and 20th century after several legislations. Goa became independent only in 1961 to be an integral part of India so colonial laws were abolished and central laws became operative in Goa. However, an exception was made to retain the family laws as these were accepted by all the communities residing in Goa. The most important provision in these family laws is regarding disposal of immovable and movable property in the event of death or divorce.

The law provides both parents to have a common right over the estate and the property has to be divided equally. Son and daughter also have equal right on the property without any discrimination. The family law in Goa provides compulsory registration of marriage which helps in checking the social evil of child marriage and bigamy. 'To strengthen the family system which is the backbone of society', was the main philosophy behind the Goa Civil Code enacted by the erstwhile rulers of Goa. This also provided a spirit of tolerance between the couple and an inbuilt safeguard for protection against injustice. Former

Chief Justice of India Y. V. Chandrachud[74] on Uniform Civil Code, reiterated that its realization is found in Goa Civil Code and hopefully one day it will awaken the rest of the country.

4.6 Conclusion:

From the above discussion it has clearly emerged out that the legislative efforts of integrating Personal laws in modern day India must be appreciated in the light of our distinct socio-religious background and historical development from medieval time to modern time. No doubt the seeds of democratization of codified Personal law were engineered during colonial time. However in the first decade following independence government of India went in a big way to bring about legislation in Hindu Personal Laws, having a far reaching influence on other religious communities to ponder upon reforms in their age old Personal laws. The key issues surrounding demand of Uniform Civil Code in fact lies in injustice to women in one form or the other in different religious communities. Slow yet conscious as well as conscientious efforts made by Indian Legislature in the direction of U.C.C., are worth appreciating in view of complex nature of our socio-religious system. That is why sometimes it appears that judicial initiative has many a time, out cornered the legislative efforts by stressing time and again the needs for enactment of a Uniform Civil Code.

---

[74] Mohd. Ahmed Khan v. Shah Bano Begum(1985) SCR(3) 844

Chapter V
Judicial trends

5.1 General:

Judiciary since post-colonial time is playing a crucial role in highlighting the need of a Uniform Civil Code by its varied pronouncements. In-fact, in a country like India, with caste and religion based politics, even after 70 years of independence to some extent due to lack of consensus on Uniform Civil Code and democratic attitude in Indian psyche, it has not been possible to bring about desired legislation so far. On the other hand, judiciary is playing a key role through its various interpretations in bringing personal laws of different communities into a single fold, thereby paving the way for Uniform Civil Code. Therefore, it is the Higher Judiciary which is viewed as being instrumental in bringing about necessary legal development in facilitating the implementability of Uniform Civil Code.

The Directive Principles of State Policy, enumerated from Articles 37 to 51 in the Constitution of India, have two distinguishing features from other provisions of the constitution. First of all, Directive Principles are not

Chapter V: Judicial Trends

justiciable in nature and hence, they cannot be enforced by Courts. This means, no remedy is available to an affected party byway of Judicial proceedings. Secondly, Directive Principles are fundamental in the governance of the country and it shall be the duty of the State to apply these principles in making laws. In Part IV of the Constitution of India, an attempt has been made as a Constitutional obligation on State to secure for its citizens a Uniform Civil Code throughout the territory of India. Various cases emanating from this Chapter have dealt with challenging the constitutionality of certain personal laws. At times Courts have expressed desirability of enactment of a Uniform Civil Code, *suo motto*. The very conception of the idea of Uniform Civil Code in the Constitution of India, since its inception, has been a topic of intense debate among the framers of the Constitution as well as various Jurists.

No Article of Directive Principles of State Policy has drawn so much attention with a great deal of controversy as 'Uniform Civil Code' under Article 44, which states that "*The state shall endeavor to secure for citizens a Uniform Civil Code throughout the territory of India*". Court cases in this regard discussed the constitutional validity of certain Personal Law whenever aggrieved group or person challenged them in Court of Law, and in a few cases, Courts have acted *Suo motto* in favor of enacting Uniform Civil Code. Before we venture further into judicial efforts and trends in the direction of implementation of a Uniform Civil Code, it would be worthwhile to look at the possibility of Uniform Civil

Code in any state of India. The Goan Model is one such example which deserves a brief mention. Goa state has enforced Uniform Civil Code for all its citizens. This is because the Portuguese Civil Code which was introduced way back in 19th century still remains in force after independence of Goa in 1961. The Uniform Civil Code in Goa is a progressive law. It permits equality of income and property irrespective of gender which includes both husband and wife as well as children. Under this law, every death, birth and marriage is mandatorily to be registered. Divorce invites severe penalty. Even Muslim whose marriage is registered in Goa cannot practice polygamy or instantaneous form of triple *talaq*. The best part of the code is that all the property and wealth owned or acquired by each spouse is jointly held by the couple. In the event of divorce each spouse is entitled for half the share of property. In the event of death of one spouse, the ownership of the remaining half of the property is vested in the other as well. According to Goa Civil Code, if married children are living independently, then the other half has to be divided equally among them. This put some kind of restrictions on parents not to disinherit the children completely as they can only dispose of half of the property they own through a will as the remaining has to be mandatorily and equally divided amongst their children. Let us now look into a few select case laws in order to appreciate the Judicial interpretation in this regard.

5.2 Narasu Appa Mali case:

In this case of State of Bombay vs Narasu Appa Mali[75], changes in Hindu Law was challenged by putting forth the argument that it is violative of Articles 14, 15 and 25 of the Constitution of India. This verdict is crucial as it laid down the extent to which Personal Laws can be subjected to the acid test of Fundamental Rights. As it involved the paramount question of how far Personal Laws can be considered "Law" within the purview of Article 13 of the Constitution. In this case, it was held that "Personal Laws" is not included in the expression "*Laws in force*" as used in Article 13(1) of the Constitution. Averments were made to justify polygamy by stating that marriage among Hindus is a part of religion being a sacramental act and having a son is regarded as spiritual benefit. However, the Court decided in favor of adoption of a son rather than allowing for a second marriage. In this landmark case, the Court left the issue of Uniform Civil Code for legislators to decide, while upholding the validity of Bombay Act Chief Justice Chagla drew inferences and heavily relied on Davis vs. Beason a US case law dealing with Idaho statute of 1882, that US federal laws against polygamy did not conflict with the 'free exercise' clause of the First Amendment to the United States Constitution. [76] Thus, the important outcome of the case was the Judicial interpretation that polygamy is not an integral part of Hindu religion. If

---

[75] State of Bombay V. Narasu Appa Mali case (AIR 1952 Bom 84)

[76] Id note 63

action of the state of Mumbai as a measure of social reform, compels Hindus to become monogamist than state is empowered to legislate under Article 25(2)(b) irrespective of the fact that it may interfere with the right of a citizen, freely to profess, practice and propagate his religion. In deciding this landmark case, the main point emerging out of the verdict is that the religious freedom guaranteed by Article 25 is the protection of religious faith and belief and not of religious practices.

Just like Bombay Act, the Madras Hindu (Bigamy and Divorce) Act 1949, was also put to a challenge on similar reason. The Court held that religious beliefs are constitutionally protected but religious practices can be regulated by the State. In addition to this, in the case of Ram Prasad vs. State of U.P., the statutory provisions prohibiting bigamy among Hindus was upheld by Allahabad High Court. Therefore, religious practice can be controlled by the legislation if, state is of the opinion that it is important in the interest of social welfare and reforms.

5.3 Shah Bano case:

Another landmark case which relates to Muslim Personal Law and Uniform Civil Code is Mohd. Ahmad Khan vs. Shah Bano Begum[77]. Historically, prominent, this was a case under section 125 CrPC at Indore. This case landed in Supreme Court for final verdict. A five-judge bench

---

[77] supra note 62

comprising the then Chief Justice Chandrachud delivered the verdict by making certain observations for Muslim personal Law and Uniform Civil Code. The Apex Court strongly condemned the Government of India for its inability to bring about enactment of Uniform Civil Code. In the instant case, Advocate Mohd. Ahmed Khan of Indore in 1975 broke his matrimonial home after 43 years of marriage by driving Shah Bano out of matrimonial home. In 1978, the Shah Bano filed a Civil Suit under Section 125 of Criminal Procedure Code in the Court of JMFC, Indore, demanding maintenance of a sum of ₹500 per month. However, on 6th November 1978, Mohd. Ahmad Khan divorced Shah Bano by using power of instant talaq and advanced the argument that she is no more his wife and he has no obligation to maintain her. He also deposited ₹3000 as dower in the Court during the period of *Iddat*. The JMFC Court in August 1979 ordered to pay ₹25 monthly for maintenance. Shah Bano aggrieved by this order, requesting for enhancement of maintenance approached M.P. High Court bench at Indore in 1980. The High Court enhanced the amount to ₹179.20/- monthly. Aggrieved by the order of the High Court her husband Mohd. Ahmad Khan appealed before the Apex Court through Special Leave Petition. The Bench before which this case was listed, referred it to be placed before the Chief Justice of India for being heard by a larger Bench as the case involved substantial question of law having far reaching consequences. A Constitutional Bench comprising of five judges, including the then C.J Chandrachud, was formed which heard the case. The Apex Court held:

- That, there is no conflict between Muslim Personal Law and Section 125 of Cr.P.C. as far as maintenance of divorce is concerned. However, in the event of conflict Section 125 Cr.P.C. shall prevail.
- That, if a Muslim husband marries another woman, his first wife has a right to refuse to live with him and entitled to get maintenance from him.
- That, women divorced has a right to get maintenance till her remarriage or death under section 125 of the Code of Criminal Procedure.
- That, the Apex Court strongly criticized the Government of India for its inability to enact Uniform Civil Code.

It was followed by intervention of All India Muslim Personal Law Board by putting forth the argument that Court has no power to interpret *Shariah* and *Quran* and it is unwarranted. This judgement infused fuel to fire and communalized the atmosphere. According to critics, it was a clear case of judicial self-restraint and the concept of Judicial Activism was much needed on such issues.

5.4 Jorden Diengdeh case:

This case, Jorden Diengdeh vs. S.S Chopra[78] of 1985, related to Christian Personal Law. Justice O. Chinapa

---

[78] Jorden Diengdeh vs. S.S Chopra of 1985

Chapter V: Judicial Trends

Reddy gave verdict, without taking into consideration the wishes of Christian community and their personal law. The brief facts of the case were that the Petitioner belongs to *Khasi* tribe of Meghalaya and was born and brought up as a Christian. She married a Sikh under the Christian Marriage Act, of 1872 in the year 1975. She filed a petition in the High Court under the provisions of Indian Divorce Act, 1869 invoking Section 19, 20 and 22 in the year 1980 for declaration to nullify the marriage or judicial separation, on the ground of impotency and sexual incompatibility with her husband. This petition was rejected by the learned single bench. The Petitioner aggrieved by this judgement, preferred a Special Leave to Appeal (hereafter SLP) in the Supreme Court. The issue before the Court was that the marriage appeared to have had broken down irretrievably, but it was not possible to give the relief under the Christian law. So, the Court expressed the necessity of enactment of a 'Uniform Civil Code'. The Court reproduced the ground of divorce and nullity under various provisions of Indian Divorce Act, 1869; Parsi Marriage and Divorce Act, 1936; Dissolution of Muslim Marriage Act, 1939; Special Marriage Act, 1954; Hindu Marriage Act, 1955 and concluded as under:

"it is thus seen that the law relating to judicial separation, divorce on nullity of marriage is, far from being uniform. Surely the time has come now for a complete reform of the law relating to marriage and make a uniform law applicable to all people irrespective of religion and caste. We suggest that the time has come for the intervention of the Legislature in these matters to

provide for a Uniform Code of marriage and divorce and to provide by law for a way out of the unhappy situations in which couples like the present have found themselves. We direct that a copy of this order may be forwarded to the Ministry of Law and Justice for such actions as they may deem fit to take"

Finally, court did not give any relief to the victim in the instant case who was left to suffer endlessly.

Thus, what Jordan Diengdeh [79] and many other case brought to sharp focus was the need for a re-codification of the age old Christian Law of 1865-1872 in India, since it is the women who are the worst sufferers of these outdated laws, perhaps owing to a patriarchal interpretation in the hands of foreign overlords.

5.5 Sarla Mudgal case:

This is yet another famous case pertaining to Personal Laws of both Hindus and Muslims. Uniform Civil Code was discussed at length in the Sarla Mudgal case[80], and Court was in favor of enactment of Uniform Civil Code. The issue before the Court were:

•Article 44 is based on the assumption that in a civilized society, between religion and personal law there is no necessary connection.

---

[79] supra note66

[80] Sarla Mudgal V. Union of India, AIR1995 SC1531

Chapter V: Judicial Trends

- Matters related to marriage, succession and like, which are of secular character, cannot be bought within Articles 25, 26 and 27 of the Constitution.
- Article 44 is a decisive step towards national integration.
- Justice Kuldeep Singh observed that the personal laws of Hindus also have a sacramental origin just as for Muslims or Christians. Hindus along with Sikhs, Buddhists and Jains have forsaken their sentiments for the cause of national unity and integration.
- The Constitution provides for a Uniform Civil Code for entire India. Justice Kuldeep Singh further to observe[81] *"Those who preferred to remain in India after the partition, fully knew that the Indian leaders did not believe in the two nation or three nation theory and that in the Indian Republic there was to be only one nation- Indian nation - and no community could claim to remain a separate entity on the basis of religion."*
- The Court directed the Government of India to immediately enact a Uniform Civil Code by introducing a Bill in the Parliament. The above observations or the *obiter dicta* of the judgement have ruined the sensible *ratio decidendi*, of the case that is to hold that the second marriage of a Hindu husband after his conversion to Islam (without getting his first marriage dissolved), as a void marriage. The ruling of the Court that majority has forsaken their personal

---

[81] supra note 68

laws for national unity met criticism on the ground that the very legislative history of Hindu Law statutes clearly indicate that these statutes were enacted for ameliorating the situation of Hindu women rather than national unity. Also, codified Hindu Law of 1955-56 was extended to three communities as they never had any scripture based personal laws. However, as far as the other communities like Muslims, Christians and Parsis are concerned they always had their own religion based Personal Laws. Not only this, a large population of Hindu tribes were allowed to follow freely their old customs and thus were kept out of the purview of Hindu Personal Law enactment of 1955-56. This situation made critics say that it was neither uniform nor free from religion and gender-based discrimination, as exceptions were made in the form of customs and caste. So according to critics, the Hindu legislation of 1955-56 was not in tune with the objectives of Article 44. It was also observed by legal scholars that the Hindu law statutes themselves do not completely satisfy the ideals of secularism, gender justice, legal equality and uniformity as envisaged in the Constitution of India. Hence, it cannot be imposed on the other communities just for the sake of Uniform Civil Code. At this point it will be appropriate to quote an Article in Sunday Observer by an eminent lawyer Indira Jaisingh:

"One of the largest beneficiaries of the absence of a Common Civil Code has been the Hindus. The Judgement in Sarla Mudgal case exposes the

hypocrisy of the Hindu community rather than the so-called backwardness of Muslim Personal Law...."

Regarding the Courts observation of "*no necessary connection between religion and personal law in a civilized society*", the scholars of Islam are of the opinion that the Islamic Law and religion under Islam cannot be separated. Regarding the institution of marriage, their view is that marriage is of the nature of both *Ibadat* or devotional act and *Muamlat* or dealings among men. So, under Islam the notion of religion covers the entire life cycle and even beyond. Some scholars are also of the view that America and other western countries, whom Indian society tries to emulate, actually pretend to practice monogamy but they practice polygamy. Therefore, in a net shell verdict in Sarla Mudgal case made observation regarding the desirability of enacting a Uniform Civil Code.

5.6 Ahmedabad Women Action Group Case:

Soon after the Sarla Mudgal case, yet another case through Public Interest Litigation, came up which raised issues regarding the Muslim Personal Law. This PIL filed by Ahmedabad Action Group[82], had a vast area of subject matter, ranging from polygamy, unilateral *talaq*, Muslim Women (Protection of Right on Divorce) Act 1986 to inheritance laws. The Apex Court, while disposing off

---

[82] Ahmadabad Women's Action Group (AWAG) v. Union of India, AIR 1997 SC 3614

this PIL, clubbed it with two other petitions filed by Lok Sevak Sang and Young Women Christian Association. However, the Court, while disposing off these cases, made an observation to restore original Constitutional position of Uniform Civil Code and left the cases for legislature to deliberate upon.

It is amply clear from above cases that, on occasions when the Constitutional validity of certain provisions relating to Personal laws was challenged on the basis of violation of fundamental rights, the courts observed self-restraint and revert the cases in legislative domain. Thus, the Courts have held an attitude that such matters lie in the domain of legislative wisdom and are matters of State policy about which Courts are not ordinarily concerned in the scheme of three organs of governance, as envisaged in the theory of separation of powers.

Regarding the Muslim Personal Law petition urged:

- To declare polygamy as void as offending Articles 14 and 15 of the Constitution.
- To declare unilateral *talaq* as void offending Article 13, 14 and 15 of the Constitution unless the consent of wife was not taken or judicial process of courts was not resorted to.
- To declare that act of polygamy is an act of cruelty within the meaning of Clause VIII(f) of Section 2 of the Dissolution of Muslim Marriages Act, 1939.

- To declare the Muslim Women (Protection of Rights on Divorce) Act abridging Article 14 and 15 of the Constitution as void.
- Sunni and Shia laws of inheritance to be declared as void as they are gender discriminating providing lesser share to women in comparison to males.

The other two petitions prayed for similar kind of relief. The Court could not decide any petition on merits because these involved issues of State policies which are to be best dealt with by Legislators as Courts are not supposed to have concerns regarding it ordinarily. Thus, Court was of the view that the remedy lies somewhere else and not by knocking at the doors of the Court and dismissed the petition by observing that "these are all matters for Legislature. The Court cannot legislate in such matters." The Court also held that a uniform law, though highly desirable, but enactment in one go may be counter-productive for the unity and integrity of India.

Therefore, the instant case was a case dealing with PIL challenging gender discrimination provisions in Muslim, Hindu and Christian statutory and non- statutory laws. In this case Apex Court adopted a conservative attitude by holding that in personal laws gender discrimination is a issue of state policy which ordinarily is not the concern of Courts. This decision mat a lot of criticism for not protecting the right to equality regarding gender issues. Similarly in Lily Thomas V. Union of India and ors,[83]AIR 2000 SC 1650 Apex Court held that importance of Uniform Civil Code cannot be denied but it needs appropriate social climate to be created by the society for its acceptance, for which statesman and leaders must rise above personal gain and awaken the masses to accept change in national interest.

In the matter of marital relationship, Law Commission of India and the Supreme Court have recommended that the legislature should bring out a separate legislation on irretrievable break down of marriage as a separate ground of divorce.

However, it is strange that on many occasions the Court undesirably resorted to judicial activism by emphasising the desirability of enactment of Uniform Civil Code. This can be attributed to the fact that Indian Judiciary was aware that in the matter of Personal Laws women are subject to injustice.

The main problem in the Hindu Law pertains to registration of marriages, which has defeated the noble purpose of preventing the child marriage. In fact, practically all religious groups in India, accept the practice of child marriage and many time they go unchecked due to non-registration of marriage.

---

[83] Lily Thomas V. Union of India and ors,AIR 2000 SC 1650

5.7 Seema V. Aswani Kumar case:

The Apex Court in Seema v. Ashwani Kumar's[84] case took a stern stand and directed all the states of the Union to frame rules for compulsory registration of marriages irrespective of religious affiliation within a time bound schedule. Non-registration of marriages in India has created a huge problem of abandoning spouses by their Non-Resident Indian husbands who reside in a foreign country. Therefore, reforms have become imperative to check the menace of child marriage, prevent marriages without consent, check bigamy, polygamy, ensure women's rights of residence, maintenance, inheritance, taking deterrent measures in deserting women by NRIs and last but not the least, checking trafficking of young girls under the guise of marriage.

5.8 Vishwa Lochan Madan V. Union of India case:

The Apex Court in famous case of Vishwa Lochan Madan v. Union of India[85] and others, issued notices to Union Government, various State Governments, All India Muslim Personal Law Board and Darul Ullom (centre of Islamic learnings at Deoband), asking them to explain the challenge posed by the very existence of parallel Islamic and Shariat Courts to Judicial System in India. The Court also categorically directed to restrain such Organization not to interfere in marital matters of Indian Muslim

---

[84] Seema V. Aswani Kumar AIR(2006)SC1158

[85] Vishwa Lochan Madan V. Union of India, (2014)7SCC707

citizens, passing judgment, remarks or fatwa. Also, under Hindu Religion similar problems of parallel Courts exist in the form of Caste Panchayats or *Khap* Panchayats. Traditionally, these *Khap* Panchayats have played a vital role at village level in number of states in India. These *Khap* Panchayats which are caste-based village councils are extra-constitutional bodies, having no recognition of law and their decisions are not enforceable by law. They are also not the elected bodies under a statute. The source of power of these *Khap* Panchayats is from community recognition. The decision of *Khap* Panchayats are often very heinous in inter-caste marital matters, leading to honor killings. Recently, Hon'ble Supreme Court has warned *Khap* system not to take law in their hand as it is unconstitutional but leave it to the courts to decide.

5.9 Shayara Bano v. Union of India case:

In this case on 22nd August 2017, a Constitutional Bench comprising of five judges of the Supreme Court with a wafer thin 3:2 majority pronounced that the practice of instantaneous Triple Talaq is unconstitutional[86]. In short, Shayara Bano was married to Rizwan Ahmed who divorced her in 2016 by practice of triple talaq (talaq-e-biddat). The petitioner aggrieved by injustice filed a a writ petition in the Apex Court demanding that three practices of talaq-e-biddat. Polygamy and nikah-halala be declared unconstitutional as they are violative of Articles 14, 15, 21 and 25 of the Constitution.

---

[86] Shayara Bano v. Union of India and others

5.10 Kantaru Rajeevaru v. Indian Young Lawyers Association and ors (Sabarimala case):

This is an interesting case challenging age-old practice of gender discrimination. Women devotees of menstruating age were not allowed to worship, due to the nature of deity (underage teenage male) in Sabarimala temple. In 1991, Kerala High Court vide its judgement legalized the above interpretation to forbade women from entering the temple. In September 2018, Apex Court[87] of India held that all Hindu pilgrims irrespective of gender can enter because difference on the basis of biological differences in sex is violative of the Constitution as it violates the right to equality under Article 14, and freedom of religion under Article 25. This verdict was followed by challenge to comply due to law and order issue. However, with Sabarimala judgement it is rightly said that "Ghost of "Narasu Appa Mali" stands tamed & exorcised.

5.11 An insight to Judicial Pronouncements and Personal Laws:

Muslim Law provides for *Mehr*, as a consideration for the performance of marriage and this amount is to be fixed at the time of marriage. This is well known that marriages under Muslim Law are a contract and in *Nikah Nama* itself the condition for registration are fulfilled. The main drawback of Muslim Law is that it doesn't provide for

---

[87]Kantaru Rajeevaru v. Indian Young Lawyers Association and ors

maintenance to wife. It is presumed that the amount decided for *Mehr* will alone take care of maintenance part. Only wife has power to waive or reduce *Mehr* not the husband. However, many provisions of Muslim Law are discriminatory against women such as Polygamy is allowed not Polyandry, *Muta* marriages by husband only, practice of instantaneous triple *talaq* enough to give divorce whimsically, for which a woman has to undergo cumbersome process. The situation is much better under Hindu Law, where Law not only provides for maintenance to wife but also procedure and grounds for divorce are same for men and women.

Indian Personal Laws create a great deal of contradiction which makes the task of Judiciary very tough in terms of deciding cases related to personal laws and Judicial review. The higher Judiciary is confronted with the fact that on one hand the Constitution recognises the existence of Personal Laws.On the other hand the very existence of Articles (14 to 19) guaranteeing equal rights in the Constitution of India, contradict the first argument. A divorce under Muslim Law meets different treatment than a divorce under Hindu law because personal laws for different religious groups are inherently unequal. By this argument, Article 15 would seem to make personal law unconstitutional. Article 15 also requires non-discrimination on the basis of sex, while Muslim Personal Law favors the men in a number of ways particularly in the matter of divorce and polygamy. Judicial interpretation is that these issues remained unresolved in

Chapter V: Judicial Trends

our Constitution and our personal laws are not consistent with morality and human rights.

We must remember that Union Parliament was directed by the Apex Court to frame a Uniform Civil Code in 1985, in a landmark case of Mohd Ahmad Khan v. Shah Bano Begum, also commonly known as Shah Bano Case. The question of solemnizing a second marriage by a Hindu husband by adopting Islam was discussed in famous case of Sarla Mudgal v. Union of India. The Court was of the view that it would amount to abuse of personal laws. It was held that such an act would amount to an offense under section 494(5) of Indian Penal Code 1960 because Hindu marriage can only be dissolved under Hindu Marriage Act of 1955 and by embracing into Islam and marrying again does not dissolve the marriage under Hindu Law. The Judiciary was of a strong opinion that it is high time for a Uniform Civil Code to be introduced and Article 44 to be taken out of cold store. The Court went further by saying that where more than 80% citizens have been brought under codified personal law, now there is no justification to keep in abeyance, the Uniform Civil Code for all the citizens in the territory of India.

Another important verdict which called for the implementation of Uniform Civil Code was a case involving a priest Mr. John Vallamatton of Kerala, who challenged the Constitutional validity of Section 118 of Indian Succession Act. This Act was applicable for non-Hindus in India. The contention raised by the Appellant was that the Section 118 is discriminatory as it imposes unreasonable restrictions on Christians for donation of their property for religious or charitable purposes by way of will. The Full Bench having heard the averments of Petitioner and Union struck down the Section as unconstitutional and directed the Union Parliament to take concrete measures to enact Uniform Civil Code. It was also reiterated that by removing such inherent contradictions, based on ideologies in personal laws, a uniform civil code will emerge to help the cause of national integration.

Nonetheless, it is a truth that all personal laws irrespective of religion are discriminatory in one way or the other on the parameters or grounds of marriage, divorce, inheritance and women's rights. In the past as per Hindu *Mitakshara* code governing succession daughters were deprived of joint heirship in parental property. It was only in the famous Lata Mittal Case of 1985 after a two-decade long court battle in Apex Court Hindu daughters could secure equal rights in ancestral property.

Similarly, long back a Christian husband had the sole right to declare his wife adulterous and divorce her. But Christian women could not seek divorce on the similar ground provided it is not supported by cruelty, bestiality and sodomy. This is an example how antiquated laws were enacted to serve and protect the British interests in the colonial time.

Christian Marriage Laws although codified, bring a unique set of challenges regarding its nationwide implementation. The law is not uniformly accepted and

Chapter V: Judicial Trends

in fact absent in certain states. Exceptions being Manipur, Travancore-Cochin, Jammu and Kashmir. However, Cochin Christian Civil Marriage Act 1095 ME and Jammu and Kashmir Christian Marriage and Divorce Act, 1957 regulate Christian marriages in Cochin and Jammu and Kashmir respectively. There is no statute regulating solemnisation of marriages among Christians in Manipur.

In the case Molly Joseph vs George Sebastian. Molly after obtaining an annulment from the Church, remarried. Due to marital issues in her new marriage she approached the civil court for her rights. Her crucial rights were lost however, since the annulment from Church did not amount to a divorce in the eyes of the law. Thus, making her subsequent marriage invalid, Supreme Court upheld the husband's plea.

In the case of Parsi Personal law if a Parsi daughter marry to a non-Parsi male, she will lose her property rights while non- Parsi wife of a Parsi husband will be entitled to only half of the husband's property. This is an issue of debate in the Parsi community. In another instance Tribal women from Maharashtra and Bihar are fighting for land right.

Amongst the recent important cases is the Goolrokh Gupta Case where Supreme Court ruled in favour of the petitioner to allow her to perform funeral ceremonies of her parents in event of their demise. Goolrokh Gupta, Parsi by birth, married a Hindu man under the Special Marriage Act, 1954. She continued to practice

Zoroastrian religion after the marriage. She was prohibited from performing the last rites of her parents by the Parsi Trust in Valsad, Gujarat.

From Judicial point of view, the Directive Principles of State Policy are not enforceable in Court of Law, but these principles are fundamental in the governance of the country and it is the duty of the State to apply these principles in making of laws. However, Courts are of the view that though Directive Principles are not justiciable, but they are as much part of the Constitution as the Fundamental Rights are and hence, deserve as much attention and importance as the Fundamental Rights draw. The Court also held that the Fundamental Rights enshrined in Part III of the Constitution must be harmonized with the Directive Principle enshrined in Part IV of the Constitution and such harmony is the basic structure of the Constitution.

Socio-legal heterogeneity is well accommodated in the Constitution of India, but it leaves the family outside the purview of Fundamental Rights. In the very early days, after the Constitution of India came into force, the High Court of Bombay and later on the Apex Court held that law in Article 13 of the Constitution does not include personal laws and hence cannot be challenged on the basis of abridging Fundamental Rights. At the same time, it categorically recognises the existence of various conflicting personal laws and expressly authorises the legislatures to convert them into state laws. Parliament and legislatures have also complied with this by making laws mostly in the case of Hindu Law than Muslim Law.

Chapter V: Judicial Trends

Apart from personal laws, there are several provisions in the Constitution of India to recognise and protect social and legal pluralism. For example, Constitution is federal in structure and recognises social, geographical, linguistic and other variants among States of the Union and hence, does not treat them all uniformly by one yard stick in all matters. It also provides for special protection to linguistics minorities and their territories. It also endeavour said to protect and conserve citizens having distinct languages, script or culture. The religious or linguistic minorities have the right to establish and administer educational institutions of their choice and to get equal grant from the State for its functioning. Scheduled Castes, Scheduled Tribes, Women, Children and socially or educationally backward classes have been given special consideration in the matter of violation of Fundamental Rights. Special safeguards and representation in Parliament, State Legislative Assembly, Panchayats, Municipalities and Cooperative Societies have been provided to the Members of Scheduled Caste/Scheduled Tribes and Anglo-Indians. Scheduled Tribes of some states have got special position by having the right to be governed by their law. Thus, the above and many other provisions in the Constitution of India are indicative of the fact that the Constitution not only preserves and supports its plurality but also assures the unity and integrity of the Nation.

It is also pertinent to mention that in Anil Kumar Mahsi case, Justice Ahmadi rightly said that the Court must adhere to self-restraint, particularly in matters relating to

Personal Laws which happen to be extremely sensitive issues in India. This verdict of the Supreme Court deserves appreciation as it shows commitment of the Indian Judiciary to the doctrine of *separation of powers* which undoubtedly is the spine of any modern democracy.

5.12 Recent Media report related to Court Verdicts:

Beside the above discussion on the judicial trends, since independence regarding the issue of Uniform Civil Code it would be worthwhile to look at the recent media reports on the issue. As per the news coverage in daily *The Hindustan Times*, [88] Hon'ble Supreme Court has pronounced judgements pertaining to society at large i.e on 22-Aug-2017, in the case of triple *talaq* or *talaq-e-biddat* or instantaneous *talaq*. Hon'ble Apex court in this case held that this practice is arbitrary as marriage can be broken whimsically without any attempt at reconciliation. Thereby, declaring it unlawful and unconstitutional. However, theory of *one nation and one code* has several challenges to come across. It creates a situation where Constitution and religious laws seem to collide. Though believers of a particular religion are free to keep their custom, but a dispute before the court of law in India should be settled on the basis of a civil code. The code of a nation must prescribe to all people equal rights and obligations and allow no discrimination or even special rights on the basis of religion, caste, gender or sex. This

---

[88] The Hindustan Times article dated 23-08-2017

will pave the way for not only real freedom of religion to an individual but also fulfil constitutional aim of a long-time awaited implementation of Uniform Civil Code. It is an irony that as long as religion-based laws will remain in operation, the conflict will remain unresolved and clergy will always accuse the court of interference whenever court deliver a verdict not acceptable to them.

In this regard an interesting article appeared in the daily newspaper, The Hindu[89], dated 22 May 2017, wherein it was reported that even the Zoroastrian thought is based on "Gender compatibility, not gender equality". According to a former Zoroastrianism Scholar, both man and woman have to recognise each other's' strength. While some Zoroastrians are of the thought that prophet Zarathustra in his sermons addressed men and women as na va nyari. Thus, as per some followers there seems to be no spiritual backing to gender discrimination that widely prevails in the community. In the daily newspaper, Times of India, dated 11 November 2018, it was reported that, the judge of family court at Bandra (Mumbai) dismissed a Jewish couple's petition for divorce by mutual consent. According to the Bombay High Court[90], Jews are regulated by their personal laws and there is no statute governing their matrimonial affairs, the Judge pronounced. In such cases the parties are to show the

---

[89] *"The conflict within: Parsis and gender rights"*, article in daily Hindu 22-05-2017

[90] *"Jews have own laws, can't decide on their divorce pleas: Mumbai High Court verdict"* dated, 11 Nov 2018

court how the marriage can be dissolved by the court on grounds of mutual consent.

In the daily newspaper, *Times of India*[91], dated 6 February 2018, it was reported that nobody has right to interfere if two adults get married: SC Bench led by Chief Justice of India Dipak Mishra said that no one, either individually or collectively, has the right to interfere in a marriage between two consenting adults.The Bench also categorically told that *Khap* Panchayats to refrain from playing the role of conscience keepers of society as the Courts will go by law and not by the tradition and *gotra* in order to ascertain the legality of a marriage.

Similarly, it was also in the news[92] that Muslim Law Board has asked grooms to take oath against instant *talaq*. This is especially important in view of the verdict of Apex Court in declaring the practice of instantaneous triple talaq as unconstitutional with direction to the Union Government to frame law on the subject to curb the menace of this arbitrary practice. Since the All India Muslim Personal Law Board (AIMPLB) failed to convince the Supreme Court last year against banning instant triple *talaq*, now it is all set to make it binding on Muslim men to commit in the the *Nikahnama* (marriage contract in Islam) that they will not use the practice. This development in the Muslim Personal Law is a result of

---

[91] "*Nobody has right to interfere if two adults get married, says SC*", Times of India, article dated 06-02-2018

[92] Ibid

Muslim Women (Protection of Right on Marriage) Bill making instant *talaq* a criminal act. All India Muslim Personal Law Board has drafted a Model *Nikahnama*, requiring the groom to give an undertaking that he will not use instant triple *talaq* to divorce his wife. There has always been the history of appeasement even at the time of Saha Bano Case of 1985. However, treating whimsical instant triple *talaq* as a form of mental cruelty on women it could have been taken care of by inserting an additional proviso in Section 498A of the Indian Penal Code to serve the purpose.

Triple *talaq* which often known as *Talaq-e-biddat* or instant *talaq* is in practice among Muslims in India, especially those belonging to *Hanafi Sunni* Islamic School of Jurisprudence. The use of Triple *Talaq* in India has been a subject of controversy and intense debate. The debate is based on questioning the issues of justice, gender equality, human rights and secularism pertaining to the practice of Triple *Talaq*. Finally, Parliament of India on 30 July 2019 declared the practice of Triple *Talaq* as illegal, unconstitutional and has made it such practice a punishable offense from 1 August 2019.

5.13 Conclusion:

On the basis of above judicial trends, it is clear that Article 44 of the Directive Principles of State Policy over the year has stirred a great deal of controversy regarding implementability of Uniform Civil Code in India. In all the cases discussed above, either the constitutionality of personal laws were challenged or the court themselves took a *sue-motto* decision in favour of Uniform Civil Code. It is a fact that on certain occasions, Judiciary was criticized for being proactive in emphasising the desirability of the enactment of a 'Uniform Civil Code'. Still, conscious efforts made by Judiciary in interpreting conflicting personal laws and creating a favorables environment to bring about a Common Civil Code at appropriate time, based on gender justice and preserving human rights cannot be denied.

Therefore, various verdict of Indian Judiciary in relation to Uniform Civil Code, so far have been situation-sensitive keeping in view of the cultural-specific circumstances. The reason for not issuing a clear-cut mandate to legislate for enacting Uniform Civil Code is due to the existence of the doctrine of separation of power, thereby leaving the issue in the legislative domain to legislate on the issue of Uniform Civil Code. Although the task of bringing such uniformity in a pluralistic system is a great challenge before legislatures of India. Nonetheless, due to the recent trend of socio-economic development in India and Judicial interpretation of age-old Personal Laws, we are coming closer to a fairer family law system than ever before.

All these examples also bring us to a very pertinent question of law i.e "how can we ensure within the Constitutional frame work gender justice and secular family laws"? This will lead to another question, "are Court competent to reform personal law"? In the recent

Chapter V: Judicial Trends

case of Aswani kumar Upadhya v. Union of India in the apex Court, it has been made clear that Court must rule on law rather than meeting out remedies. In the light of the triple talaq verdict, Aswani Kumar approached to apex Court to declare the discriminatory practices of Polygamy and *Nilay halala* as unconstitutional. We must appreciate that the Religion under the Constitution, has two components one what comprises of "belief" and another what comprises of "custom". Here former is protected as a fundamental right of faith and worship under Article 25 & 26 of the Constitution of India, while the later as Personal law being immune from a fundamental right violation since it doesn't come under the purview of Article 13. However, a careful reading of Article 25 and 26 reveals that the right to faith and worship is subject to others safeguards of public safety and health, and hence not absolute. The "Personal law" on the other hand is omnipotent. Since 1951 Courts have kept away from Personal law reforms, relying on Narasu Appa Mali case that Personal law are not amenable to a writ jurisdiction. This discussion raises yet another question of law that how Court should deal with Personal laws as *Lex Lata* (as it is) or *Lex Ferenda* (as it should be)? This leaves us at a very deplorable turn in this age of scientific and technological awakening where, personal law seems to be immune from the rule of law. No doubt Religion must have absolute freedom in the matter of conscience (Article 25 & 26), but how it can be permitted to play havoc with the civil rights of people within the same faith? As law go by common prudence so if Personal law are adversely affecting the civil rights of the people following it, then it should be amenable under the rule of law. Also, in western democracies Personal law is not allowed to have the ability to affect the civil rights that's how it avoids close encounter with the law of the land. In this context Indian model is irksome as we believe in the "salad-bowl theory" rather than "melting pot theory". Therefore, creation of parity and equability within each personal law is a *sine-qua-non* for the emergence of a common civil code. The Bombay High Court in State of Bombay verses Narasu Appa Mali had held that Personal laws are not laws or laws in force under Article 13. This 1951 verdict was never challenged in the Supreme Court. The custom or usage cannot be excluded from law in force. This verdict places Personal law on equal footing with Fundamental Rights is not a good precedent, since it curtails the rule of law in a society where Constitution is held supreme.

Although Supreme Court has held differing views regarding the question of supremacy between Personal law and Fundamental right. While in some cases such as Krishna Singh Vs Mathura Ahir of 1980, Maharishi Avdesh of 1994 and Ahmedabad Women Action Group Case of 1997 the Apex Court held that Personal law could not be challenged for being in contravention of the provisions of Fundamental rights as Fundamental right could not be the touchstone to test Personal laws, while in others such as Mudaliar case of 1956 a three judge bench of Apex Court held that Personal laws are void to the extent that they are in violation of the fundamental

Chapter V: Judicial Trends

right. Therefore, basic rights are supreme being the natural right.

The situation in India is grim as Personal laws are codified as well as uncodified, existing from age old Custom and practice. In famous Mary Roy Case of 1986 relating to Christian Personal law, Apex Court held that Syrian Christian women were entitled for equal share in their father's property. In Danial Latifi Case who was the Lawyer of Shah Bano and won a maintenance claim for her in Apex Court in the year 1985. This verdict of Apex Court was against the interest of the orthodox segment of Muslim society. In order to appease the the swelling sentiments of the community, the then Rajiv Gandhi government enacted the Muslim Women (Protection of Rights on Divorce) Act 1986. This Act defeated the verdict of Apex Court by providing that a man was required to pay maintenance to divorced wife only during the period of *iddat* (90 days). Danial Latifi approached the Apex Court to challenge the Constitutional validity of the Personal law. The Apex Court in 2001, held that the Muslim Women (Protection of Rights on Divorce) Act 1986 is not violative of the Constitution or Fundamental Rights. The apex court held that Personal Law need not be tested on the touchstone of the Fundamental Rights.

In 2014, Apex Court delivered a landmark verdict on the question of adoption child by a Muslim woman since Muslim Personal law does not provide right to adopt children to a woman. A three-judge bench of the apex Court held that the Muslim women can legally adopt children like any other Indian women. Thus, the right to adopt children could not be denied by Personal law. In the year 2015, Apex Court has also rendered verdict regarding the right of unwed Hindu Mother. Under the Hindu Minority and Guardianship Act of 1956, father is held as natural guardian of a Hindu Child. In case a child is born out of wedlock, only then the mother could be considered a natural guardian. But in 2015 Apex court held that the consent of the biological father is not necessary for an unwed mother to legally become the sole guardian of a child. The Apex Court was of the view that father could not have a preferential right over the mother in matter of guardianship. These verdicts show the changing nature of Indian society, the society has evolved. But the law is evolving on case-to-case basis after long legal battles. This should leave an important thought in the mind of reader, in the present day is there a need for norms to play a role other than a cultural identity for a culture or to what degree should culture or religion be allowed to play a role in civil life of people?

Chapter VI
Conclusion and Suggestions

6.1 Conclusion:

There are diverse views on the issues of marriage, divorce, succession, inheritance and maintenance for inclusion in Uniform Civil Code among the various communities in India. India being a secular state and also the largest democracy in the world, automatically creates a need for the codification of its various age-old personal laws into a modern civil code on democratic pattern, whereby the fundamental rights of its citizens are protected equally. This is a challenge for India and its democratic values.

The debate surrounding Uniform Civil Code cannot reach a logical conclusion by placing minority rights and women's rights in opposition to each other or on the fault lines of *Hindutva* and secularism. We must understand that "uniform" does not imply common, and our experience of last few decades teach us that it is quite possible to enact reasonable uniform rights and duties through regimes of law. This is becoming possible today due to the trend of disintegration of orthodox religious authorities, growing debate and dissent within communities, and increased literacy and awareness among women.

Different aspects of Uniform Civil Code are revealed from above discussion, goal behind Article 44 and the Judicial pronouncements. India is a secular country and its Preamble declares *"liberty of thought, expression, belief, faith and worship"* read with Article 25 provided for this purpose, reads *"freedom of conscience and free profession, practice and propagation of religion"*. However, it is important to understand that in the event a of conflict or a choice, national interest is always, paramount compared to religious interest. There are arguments in favor of Uniform Civil Code on the ground of secular state, single citizenship, single tax structure, etc. Today the whole world is fast growing into a global village and uniformity needs to prevail. This poses a very pertinent question regarding the logic of the existence of different communities in such a scenario? In Indian context, Uniform Civil Code is basically an attempt to replace the age old personal laws based on the scriptures, traditions, usages and customs of each major religious group by a uniform set of rule governing every citizen so that they can enjoy being a member of human race, realizing fully their human rights as well as fundamental rights enshrined in the Constitution of India. However, these laws are distinct as compared to public law and contain issues like marriage, divorce, inheritance, adoption and maintenance governing the citizens of a nation uniformly.

Chapter VI: Conclusion and Suggestions

We are all human beings, proud to be Indian and we all have similar rights under the Constitution of India, but we are governed by different set of personal laws and at times feel helpless in empowering women belonging to certain community who live under deplorable condition and deprived of basic human rights.. Women community as such is living under double standards as women in some communities are not only enjoying more rights but are also becoming more and more powerful, while situation is not so good in other communities. It appears that time is ripe that all communities in India should be governed by the same civil laws. Therefore, enacting Uniform Civil Code is not only the need of the hour but the State also needs to reform or put an end on inconsistent laws which discriminate women on the basis of their religion. In this connection special attention needs to be drawn regarding Constitutional provisions of Article 51A(e), whereby under fundamental duty it is mentioned that to promote harmony and the spirit of common brotherhood amongst all the people of India transcending religion, linguistic, and regional or sectional diversities; to renounce practice derogatory to the dignity of women. Therefore, Article 44 and Article 51-A(e) are supportive of each other as far as gender equality is concerned which is the very purpose of enacting UCC.

The very purpose in the mind of the framers of Constitution, behind creating Article 44 was to achieve the greater objective of National Integration. Apex Court has also categorically mentioned on many occasions that

Article 44 of our Constitution has remained a dead letter. It is believed that a Uniform Civil Code will serve the greater cause of national integration by setting aside desperate loyalties to laws having conflicting ideologies. No doubt it is the duty of the State and also the test of the legislative competence to work for the enactment of much awaited Uniform Civil Code for the citizens of the country. In fact, it will bring justice to all which is the best way of dispensing Justice rather than Justice in case to case.

It may be the right time for the Nation as a whole to decide with democratic maturity to accept the Uniform Civil Code in civil matters such as marriage, succession, divorce, inheritance etc. In the larger interest of the nation, all communities have to come up with more open attitude than ever before for accepting this change. It is not against *Shariah* because most of the Muslim countries including Pakistan and 21 others have amended their personal laws by abolishing triple talaq.

It is also a time for initiating nationwide debate on good and bad provisions of existing personal laws which need to be incorporated or deleted. For example— concept of *Mahr*, proposal and acceptance of marriage from Muslim Law, monogamy, right to property of women from Hindu Law, etc could be incorporated. Similarly, scholars of law, social workers, political thinkers and religious leaders need to converge and deliberate upon the issue to find out an amicable solution for framing of the much-awaited Uniform Civil Code. It is going to be a time-consuming process which is inevitable keeping in view of our ambitions of superseding fundamentalism and religious fanaticism of all types as a nation. With the adoption of Uniform Civil Code, the irrational belief of religious superiority or religious differentiation will wane. Uniform Civil Code could emerge as a great unifying force for India. The provision of Article 44 was enacted to promote unity and integrity in a newly independent India as a cherished goal enshrined in the Preamble to the Constitution. Hindu Law of marriage underwent tremendous reformative changes in mid-fifties, but it met resistance from Muslim community. In a bid to avoid this resentment, Government in power exhibited a lack of political will to enforce Uniform Civil Code.

So it can be easily inferred that, on several occasions, Hon'ble Supreme Court, having settled the ambiguity and controversy arising out of apparent conflicts among various personal laws, has stressed the necessity of enacting a Uniform Civil Code. Had Uniform Civil Code been implemented timely then there would have been no need of filing so many civil cases and need for the Apex court by interpreting various Personal Laws. It would have also kept the communal divisive forces at bay by ushering in an era of communal harmony and national integration. However, it cannot be denied and ignored that the personal laws in India are varied in their very source, philosophy and applicability. The major problem is of gathering people governed by different religious groups on a common platform. Just like in most modern nations, a Uniform Civil Code will strive to administer the same civil laws on all citizens, irrespective of their caste, religion or tribe. There is no denying the fact that the Constitution of India deliberately enumerated certain Directive Principles of State Policy with the sole objective to ameliorate socio-economic condition of the masses. This is with a view to promote welfare of the people in order to achieve economic democracy. One such Directive is Uniform Civil Code under Article 44, which is considered fundamental to the governance of the country. This is clear that the mandate of the Article 44, is addressed to "state" which invariably takes into its ambit the Government and Parliament of India and the Government and Legislative Assembly of all the States including all other local and Municipal bodies and other bodies under the Government of India. This was the wisdom of the framers of our Constitution, who could anticipate the issue related to such a piece of legislation in times to come. This is why the wording like "enact" was avoided and plain words like "endeavour

" and "strive" were inserted in Article 44. The founding fathers of the Constitution of India, right in the aftermath of widespread violence and riots in 1947 as a result of partition, were matured enough by the experience and hence were not in a haste. They wanted to give a time space amongst different religions and communities to mature and later on get amalgamated by adopting a Uniform Civil Code voluntarily. So, the very expectations of the framers of the Constitution were that Uniform Civil Code be enacted and enforced as a result

Chapter VI: Conclusion and Suggestions

of an evolutionary process post-independence, whereby Indian society has matured to accept voluntarily the Uniform Civil Code as a part of their civil life.

India as a nation is known to be a land of cultural diversity, multiple languages and religions. Since time immemorial *unity in diversity* has been the characteristic feature of India as a nation. However, in the contemporary time where the world is on the verge of becoming a global village due to the process of globalisation, uniformity in the law has become a need. Also, we must not forget that since 1950 the Indian Constitution has undergone transformation in the form of various Amendments. So far, 124 Amendments have been made under Article 368, without abridging the basic structures of the Constitution. These Amendments on one hand exhibit that Indian Constitution is not only a living document, but it also caters to the needs and aspiration of its people in a fast-changing time. That is to say, the Indian Constitution is a rigid yet a flexible document. Talks on Uniform Civil Code are going on since independence and Constitutional Assembly Debate time. During the debate, due to lack of consensus to arrive at a common ideology, the Article was reduced to Directive in nature rather than mandatory. This is how an attempt was made in Article 44, to empower the State with this responsibility. Today, India has achieved a uniform legislation in almost every sphere of national life (civil, contractual, criminal etc) except family and matrimonial laws. The judiciary, through various pronouncements, has been playing a proactive role to highlight the need for a Uniform Civil Code. This has been criticized as Judicial Overreach, but it has also found appreciation by Indian masses of varied background. The Supreme Court has asked Union Government regarding its willingness to enact a Uniform Civil Code, in order to override age old inconsistent personal laws of different religious groups. Despite the heated debate on Uniform Civil Code one thing is undisputed and that is any provision of personal law that abridges or violates the Fundamental Rights stands unconstitutional as per Article 13, in Part III of the Constitution and hence it must be struck down. Besides this, inherent inconsistency in various personal laws has also been challenged on the grounds of Article 14, which guarantees the Right to Equality. It is evident that the highest judicial authority in India and the constitutional mandate envisaged by the forefathers seem to be pointing towards a change, one that was foreseen but has been long forgotten. Perhaps to be a more cohesive and a vibrant nation the time may have come to fulfil the Constitutional commitment of Uniform Civil Code under Article 44, thereby bringing in its ambit a large number of personal laws.

Despite the active efforts by the Judiciary, it is a prime responsibility of the Union Parliament to enact Uniform Civil Code, but governments are often inclined towards political considerations and deterred by communal intolerance. In the recent history of Indian politics, most political parties kept their lips tight on this issue while the BJP Government had Uniform Civil Code, in their election agenda of 2014. Today BJP and like-minded organizations are working together in this direction. In this regard example of Goa could shed light on the path being the only State in India practicing Article 44, also known as the Goa Civil Code, collectively known as Family Laws.

There are several problems concerning Uniform Civil Code, such as its relationship with secularism, different views on marriage, divorce and maintenance, how to integrate personal laws without hurting the religious sentiments of various stake holders, and need for codification, etc. The main controversy surrounding the Uniform Civil Code has been secularism and the freedom of religion guaranteed by the Constitution of India. India as a nation has no State-owned religion and state is not concerned with the relation of man with God. As a secular State, it is only concerned with the relation between man and man and there is no room for discrimination on the ground of religion. Religion is only perceived as imparting the righteous way of life in Indian context. Therefore, enactment of a Uniform Civil Code is possible by maintaining a delicate equilibrium between various personal laws, customs and common law governing Indian citizens.

On the basis of the critical analysis of various literature available and study conducted, the question of U.C.C. as an instrument for religious unity is likely to receive some backlash and negativity from the people initially. This is inevitable due to our historical context of cultural riots, communal tension and religious differences which unfortunately still persists even after 70 years of independence in India. Another reason relates to the failure of governance, failure in strict adherence to rule of law, the due process of law and transparency in the administration, which remain at large even after 70 years of independence. Beside all this, the lack of political consensus among various political and religious groups due to their vested interest, vote bank politics even sometimes on matters of national importance, is a challenge of the Indian Polity. Here it is pertinent to mention that the indian polity seems to be divided over commitments to their voters (promises) and bringing about Directive Principle related endeavors. The quick results fetching commitments to voters owing to the myopic issues take the centre stage in day-to-day politics while the nation building and transformative tasks such as the U.C.C. get sidelined owing to inherent slow results. Which need a deep ideological deliberation from the legislatures. A deliberation that may be too far-fetched for any legislator to ponder on, as it would require the understanding of not only the ground situation but a great deal of socio-legal matters. In this light, citizen awareness could go a long way in ascertaining better law makers from amongst themselves. Also, the faith of the people has to be reinforced in the legislatures to be the bearer of social change.

The Indian society is aware of the existence of various personal laws, this lays down the foundation of existence of differences in these practices. This foundation could play a key role in acknowledging the need for an accepted

Chapter VI: Conclusion and Suggestions

uniformity across cultures. As part of a single civilization, though uniformity brings ease of justice along with speed, it also brings the question of religious restriction for some. A restriction that may appear to threaten the cultural diversity, visa-vie a deterrent to change. Here, the onus of change falls on the government and advocates of the change, to engage in countless dialogues to bring the respective stakeholders onboard, to redress and clarify the extent of change. Therefore, without spreading awareness among the masses about the advantages of a Uniform Civil Code, smooth transition of integrating various personal laws may not be possible. The mass ignorance of Uniform Civil Code in India is the core reason for the cynicism regarding the matter, without the awareness it will continue to be perceived as a threat.

It may be a matter of debate from a legal perspective whether different religious communities should be allowed different conflicting personal laws, particularly with respect to basic human rights, a constitutional mandate. But from a sociological perspective, in a modernising democracy like India, marriages among different caste and religion can lead to social tension. Modernisation has galvanized a social change, inter-caste and inter-religion marriages are now inevitable part of Indian society. With a new galvanized society, India still has to depend on its age-old personal laws to protect the interests of its citizens. Therefore, in modern day parlance society has to rise above the constraints of caste, religion and color. This will pave the way for a better national integration, and a more cohesive social order. A social order, that could find its strength with the U.C.C. as its very backbone.

India is a unique nation with presence of various codified personal laws of different religious groups. So many religious communities co-exist in India but there exists no uniform family law for all Indians, which is acceptable to them. The guiding doctrine is to treat every individual on equal footing and to protect them all by just, fair and predictable laws. The very inconsistency in various personal laws in India serves as a breeding ground to perpetuate social injustice and gender discrimination. Therefore, it is important to ensure that every human being is treated with dignity which they rightly deserve by virtue of being a member of human race. Society is in a dynamic flux of change with time and so the laws governing personal aspects need a change to suit the need and aspirations of today. Due to rapid globalisation process, every aspect of human and national life is undergoing a rapid transformation i.e education, economy, technology, agriculture, social outlook, work culture, lifestyle, etc. Even due to technological breakthrough, in this age of internet, the communication gap between rural areas and urban areas is shrinking very fast. This transformation is paving the way for breaking the shackles of obsolete customary and superstitious beliefs in family matters. This transformation brings society no matter how far flung to the shore of change. Todays' reduced distances carry the wave of a collective change. Thanks to technology, melting pot is not just a regional phenomenon, now in many ways it is a global phenomenon. Thus, a Uniform Civil Code will help in changing the perception of millions of people regarding how families are governed within the existing democratic set up. Uniform Civil Code is not a distant reality in the current socio-political scenario of India. Special Marriage Act of 1954 is an example of secular legislation, which allows and governs the union of two individuals irrespective of their religious affiliation. It is appropriate to mention here what Justice Y.V Chandrachud, remarked, *"a common civil code will help in strengthening the cause of national integration by removing conflicting interests"*.

Believers of the theory of legal pluralism argue that the very concept of uniformity is forced while that of Diversity is natural. As per Hobbes, people lived by their own group norms, as state of nature, these group norms may vary from group to group in one aspect or other. Hobbes conceived the idea of a sovereign to whom all people expressed their allegiance in exchange for establishing an order. Austin used a new concept to define law in top-down terms that all law was direct or indirect command of the sovereign and whatever could not be so proved could not be law. Later on, scholars like Kelsen and Hart gave a bottom-up description of all laws by propounding that any norm or rule of conduct to be a law must be capable of being traced back to a grundnorm or rule of recognition. Unless it is capable of being so traced, it is not a law. However, from 1930 onwards, many legal scholars including Ehrlich, started questioning the concept of law. The very basis of questioning was the difference between the state law and people's behaviour noticed by these scholars. In fact, people perceived and also practiced a lot of things which either have no connection with the State law or even if there was any connection, people behaved in such a flexible manner that they did not come in conflict with the state laws. This is how over the years people have indulged in a lot of activities by forming clubs or religious groups or association or any other informal organisation without coming in conflict with State laws, even till date. In fact, the very norm set by these groups or bodies were such that they were highly respected as well as voluntarily accepted by all so that they could regulate large part of their lives without State intervention and at times even larger than regulated by State laws. It was initially all societies lived like that as per their customary laws. We cannot deny the fact that even after the establishment of the State they continued to live like that except criminal acts for which the same law applied to all e.g penal code.

In view of above discussion and the context of Uniform Civil Code, it is worthwhile to ponder upon the theoretical work of French philosopher physicist Louis-De Broglie on the concept of nature of light, i.e is it a wave or particle? De Broglie is known for propounding the theory of wave-particle duality which means that the light or all types of radiations are both particle as well as wave that means light at times behaves like a wave and at times as a particle i.e (it is wavicle in nature). The argument behind this concept is that though the nature loves diversity but at the same time it also loves symmetry e.g all leaves of a tree cannot be absolutely identical, but they are symmetrical and same connection can be discovered everywhere in nature. So, following this reality of nature in our diversified society, we can surely locate some symmetry in our personal laws which will pave the way for unification of various personal laws, yet retaining their unique features. The result will be a *Symmetrical Civil Code*, taking care of human rights, gender justice and removing all forms of discrimination.

At the same time, we must remember that the Constitutional commitment, i.e *"to promote harmony and the spirit of common brotherhood amongst all the people of India transcending religious, linguistic and regional or sectional diversities"*, a fundamental duty entrusted by the Constitution of India to all the citizens. Thus Article 44 of the Directive Principles of State Policy is expected to be harmonized with this duty. The consensus among different communities about aforementioned duty alone can trigger the process of realisation of Uniform Civil Code. Therefore, any attempt to realise the goal of Uniform Civil Code will be unsuccessful as long as a consensus is not reached among the communities.

It is also important to remember that secularism is a basic feature of the Constitution of India. The Constitution, guarantees Indians equality in its Preamble and also in other provisions including Articles 14-18 in Part III. Thus, the Constitution envisages a cohesive, unified and casteless society.

It is also worthwhile to note that the Islamic teachings also include two important socio-moral Principles that of gender justice and social equality. It was Prophet who declared that women could inherit property and that a wife's asset belonged solely to her. Not to mention, it was the time when girl children were being buried alive at birth. All human beings are equal is the very essence of Holy *Koran*. The above argument brings us to a very important conclusion that no one should have qualms about accepting a well-founded model of Uniform Civil Code which promotes gender Justice and social equality and does not discriminate on the basis of religion or caste.

Keeping in view of the historical background of various personal laws, legislative efforts made in this direction with the proactive role played by Judiciary being the custodian of the Indian Constitution from time to time would act as a check and balance. This also goes without saying that, the intricacies addressed as a result of a fruitful debate on the issues surrounding UCC by intelligentsia and stakeholders would be the hallmark of democracy in spirit. The debate pertaining to religious norms and family laws becomes furthermore interesting when examined in the light of Normative Pluralism vs. Legal Pluralism. Tension buildup between democratic demands for the application of religious norms and human right concerns, particularly pertaining to the rights of women and children. Tensions among the competing stake holders of public policy and Legislation often come to focus in a pluralistic society due to multiplicity of exclusive claims of religious truth and visions of public

Chapter VI: Conclusion and Suggestions

good. It has been the primary function of politics in every state to deal with such disputes and controversies and resolve them through the process of mediation by compromise and accommodation. The ability of the state to mediate and adjudicate such controversies amicably in an orderly fashion decides the peace, tranquility, stability and overall well-being of a society. The prospects of political stability and social justice becomes better if proponents of each side to a controversy perceive their stand as open to negotiation and compromise. Experience has taught us that there are two complementary approaches to defuse such deadlock arising out of family matters. First approach is to re-examine the normative assumptions of a religious group of believers to see whether almighty did indeed ordain or mandate the particular view one is asserting. Another approach is to address and amicably settle such dispute by community centered mediation, instead of coercive enforcement of one view or another by the state apparatus.

Law and Society are never static and are always in a state of evolution resulting in a change from time to time. In this regard state may also influence social change by facilitation of internal cultural transformation, provided it is not perceived as an excessive or coercive step by local actors. For example, theft is a crime as well as sin. Here it is neither a sin because it is a crime, nor is it a crime because it is a sin. State stands benefited from the religious sanction of theft as a sin in order to legitimize the crime and its subsequent punishment among believers.

Some scholars are of the opinion that the normative quality of religious principles is derived from a religious frame of reference and authority outside the state institutions. State laws that operate in state courts and its institutions are political will of the people, personal laws on the other hand find their source in religious normative system. Therefore, a clear differentiation in theory and practice is required between the nature of the code of a religious normative system and state law as a secular political system.

The methodological and normative similarities between a religious code and state law and the very fact that they both intend to regulate human behavior (often in the same social space), implies the possibility of interaction and cross fertilization between these two systems. Methodologically, religious code of various communities evolved outside of the state institutions and among religious scholars and their communities, but the methods used by these scholars for developing principles and rules are similar to modern techniques of textual construction, reasoning by analogy and precedent[93]. Besides this, it is interesting to note that in the matter of property, contracts and civil liability for damage, normative similarities can be seen between a religious code and state law in general. Thus, through "civic reason" one can envision a dynamic process of mutual interaction between religious code and state law principles. Therefore, firstly religious

---

[93] Wafl. B. Hallam, sharia, theory, practice, transformations 100-10 (2009)

community has to conform with its religious normative principles without coming into conflict with the state. Secondly, it is expected that ethical values, priorities and interest of the religious majority must be reflected in state laws and administration of justice while safeguarding the Constitutional / human rights of the minority. In-fact legislation consistent with ones' religious belief through civic reason and democratic process should be adopted. Thus, enactment of Uniform Civil Code is nothing but an expression of gender justice and equality before law.

6.2 Suggestions:

Drafting of Uniform Civil Code and its implementation even after obtaining consensus will be a challenging problem and may remind us of some challenges faced by the framers at time of drafting the Constitution of India. The other important issue will be whether Uniform Civil Code should be a blend of all personal laws or a new legislation strictly based on Constitutional mandate. The time is ripe to draft a model law for adoption of Uniform Civil Code and release it in public domain for valuable suggestion. This candid step will also wipe out the very apprehension from the mind of the society, especially for whom in the disguise of Uniform Civil Code a Hindu law may be imposed. Therefore, a new code based on gender equality, containing the best elements from all personal laws will have to be looked into.

It is also important to understand that any endeavor to address U.C.C. must focus on family laws of all religions and diversity of their customary practices. It must also aim at addressing social injustices instead of plurality of laws. Thereby responding to the inevitable social change. In a fast globalizing world women's rights, inter-alia family law reforms must be perceived as an end in itself rather than a matter of Constitutional provision, political debate and religious rights.

Historically religion has been a source of tremendous unification of society rather than its division on the basis of the basic tenant of all the religion. Today unifying or divisive role of religion is a topic of intense debate nationwide. History of evolution of different religion is different as they are the product of their own space and time. Religion on time scale are still evolving. The pertinent question is that what went wrong in not adopting U.C.C. in India despite of Constitutional commitment and Judicial interpretation in a fast modernizing Indian society? The real constraints in adopting U.C.C. is not the religion itself but the selective interpretation of religion by our religion-political leaders of different religion having vested interest. The narrow-minded approach of religion is based on their feeling of superiority of their religion over others and selfish motives thereby keeping the people of different faith remain divided. This has led to indoctrination of a large segment of people of different faith and belief and is the root cause of various problems in our society today. Beside this religion is individualistic notion and mixing of religion with politics has threatened the unifying fabric of our society. It is for such leaders to

Chapter VI: Conclusion and Suggestions

understand the real essence of all the religion for a more cohesive social order.

Only through modern education by creating a broader secular outlook and in depth understanding of the people about the basic tenant of religion can help in unifying society at large. This process will narrow down the gap created among the people of different faith and belief on one hand and on the other hand will free the people from the shackles of ills of the society. After this type of maturity in society, it will be the right time for implementation of U.C.C. in India.

Keeping in view of the above, for attaining the objective enshrined under Article 44 of the Constitution of India, a multi-pronged approach could go a long way. Envisioning a UCC with these two parts may address some of the legit community concerns, bringing a greater transparency and democracy. Under UCC Part A, focus will be to form legal religious bodies to identify personal laws of various communities, with an expert panel of religious scholars and religious heads. Thus, in essence the Part A affects individual lives. Along the same lines, a UCC Part B based on Parsi model that provisions formation of trusts for regulation of religious spaces. A Cultural body that can review the constitution of these trusts and weigh rules relating to regulation of religious spaces based on historical/religious facts. Thus, UCC Part B would affect religious spaces. These two Parts will therefore act together to ascertain rights of Indian citizens individually and spatially (in religious spaces) making legal entities that can be party to a resolution process. Bringing potentially a greater accountability to an otherwise a case basis process.

However, formation of such an entity alone would not solve social issues that the authors have felt need to be addressed. Beside the above following measures need to be addressed:

- Through education, awareness and sensitization campaigning, a broadminded outlook needs to be created among the people of India to comprehend the very sprit of Uniform Civil Code.
- A National Committee comprising of eminent jurists, social workers, political thinkers and religious leaders, who are undisputed and capable of influencing the masses, needs to be constituted to maintain uniformity, so that community sentiments are taken well care off.
- The draft legislation to take out the best from every personal law and it must be open to nationwide debate so that it acts in the best interest of all the religions for its amicable acceptance. This will be mutually beneficial to all and will take within its ambit the nobble objective of to live with dignity thereby leaving no room for gender discrimination.
- More research is imperative on various aspects of Uniform Civil Code in order to understand the modalities in which family Law reforms could be introduced in the most cohesive manner, without

Chapter VI: Conclusion and Suggestions

compromising diversity and plurality which form the very core of India's social fabric.

• Teaching of good virtues and humanitarian aspect of all the religions, fostering national integrity and fraternity, must be the part of the curriculum at school and undergraduate level as a long-term measure.

Therefore, a long-awaited commitment under Article 44, of Directive Principle of State Policy in the Constitution of India will not only ensure Gender Equality but will also bring religious conflicts to an end. The application of Uniform Civil Code will help in promoting national unity, integrity, fraternity in a modern state.

References:

Books:

- Aiyar. Krishnamurthi. S Revised by H.D.Kohli, Law of Marriage, Maintenance, Separation and Divorce (3rd Edition 2010) Universal Law Publishing Co. Pvt. Ltd
- Asam A. A. Fyzee, A Modern Approach to Islam (2nd Edition 2008) Oxford University Press
- B.M Gandhi, Sumeet Malik, Hindu Law (4th Edition 2016) Eastern Book Company Lucknow
- Desai S. A, Mulla Principals of Hindu Law (20th Edition 2007) Lexis Nexis
- Dr Kahmashan.Y. Danyal, Muslim Law of Marriage, Divorce and Maintenance (2015) Regal Publications Rajouri Garden Delhi
- Dr. Paras Diwan, Modern Hindu Law (23rd Edition 2016) Allahabad Law Agency
- Gandhi, B.M. (ed), V.D Kulshrestha's landmark in Indian legal and Constitutional history, eighth edition, 2005.
- H.L.A. Hart, The concept of law (1961)
- Hans Kelsen, A general theory of law and state (1949)
- Hidayatullah M and Hidayatullah Arshad, Mulla Principals of Mahomedan Law (19th Edition 2010) Lexis Nexis

References

- Jain, M.P, Indian Constitutional law (6th Edition 2010)
- John Austin, The province of jurisprudence determined (1832)
- Justice R.K Aggarwal Revised by Prof. Dr. H. H Singh, Hindu Law, (25th Edition 2016) Central Law Agency
- M.B. Hooker, legal pluralism- An introduction to colonial and neither- colonial laws (1975)
- Menski. Werner. F, Hindu Law Beyond Tradition and Modernity (3rd impression 2010) Oxford University Press
- Mitra Partha pratim, Muslim Laws in India: contemporary issues and challenges (2015) We Books ys Book International
- Panday J.N, Constitutional law of India C. L. A Allahabad
- Prof. V. P. Bharatiya, Syed Khalifa Rashid's Muslim Law (5th Edition 2009) Eastern Book Company
- Ramesh Chandra Nagpal, Modern Hindu Law (2nd Edition 2008) Eastern Book Company
- Rawals John, A Theory of Justice (6th Edition 2013) Universsl Law Publishing Co.Pvt. Ltd. New Delhi
- Saxena Poonam Pradhan, Family Law Lectures Family Law II (2nd Edition 2007) Lexis Nexis
- Shukla, VN., Constitution of India, 201, (M.P. Singh Ed., Lucknow: Eastern Book Company, Vol. 2, 1999)
- Sir Dinshaw Fardunji Mulla, Revised by Prof. Iqbal Ali khan, Mulla Principals of Mohammedan

Law(20th Edition 2013) Lexis Nexis
- The Constituent Assembly Debates, Volume VII, NOV-23-194

Research Work:

Chavan Nandani, Kidwai, (2006). Personal Law Reform and Gender Empowerment: A Debate on Uniform Civil Code. Hope India Publication.
- Salim Akhtar and Ahemad Naseem, Personal Laws and Uniform Civil Code, p.39(1998).
- Tahir Mahmood, Personal laws in crisis, p.3(1986)
- Zafar Ahmad, personal Laws and Constitution of India: A study in contemporary

Legal dimension (2017) perspective with special Reference to Dr B.R Ambedkar, p.30 (unpublished, 1992)

Dr Parminder Kaur, Personal laws vis-a-vis UCC (2011)

Chintaman Rout, UCC and gender Justice (2013)

Alka Bharti, UCC in India - still a distant dream (2013)

Asha Rani, A term paper on UCC (2016)

V.R. Sathya, Constitutional history of India on UCC (2015)

Lepakshi Rajpal and Mayank Vats, UCC and its

References

Statutes:

- Hindu Succession Act, 1956
- The Dissolution of Muslim Marriages Act, 1939
- The Muslim Women (Protection of Rights on Divorce) Rules, 1986
- Christian Marriage Act, 1872
- Muslim Women (Protection of right on Divorce) Act, 1986
- The Code of Criminal Procedure 1973
- The Constitution of India, 1950
- The Hindu Adoption and Maintenance Act, 1956
- The Hindu Marriage Act, 1955
- The Hindu Minority and Guardianship Act, 1956
- The Muslim Personal Law (Shariat) Application Act, 1937
- The Parsi Marriage and Divorce Act, 1936
- The Special Marriage Act, 1954.

Journals:

- Academy Law Review
- Aligarh Law Journal
- All India Reporter
- Amity Law Review
- Delhi Law Review
- Indian Journal of Legal Studies
- Journal of Constitutional and Parliamentary studies
- Journal of Indian Law and Society
- Journal of Indian Law Institute
- Law Commission of India, Fifteenth Report, 1960

Magazines:

Newspapers:

- The Combat Law
- The Front Line
- The India today
- The Law Teller
- The Outlook
- The Political and Law Time

- The Danik Jagran
- The Hindu
- The Hindustan Times
- The Indian Express
- The Times of India